DENIED
DETAINED
DEPORTED

STORIES FROM THE DARK SIDE OF AMERICAN IMMIGRATION

ANN BAUSUM

WITH A POEM FOREWORD BY NAOMI SHIHAB NYE

NATIONAL GEOGRAPHIC

WASHINGTON, D.C.

For the immigrant in all of us, and for Jennifer, with thanks.

COVER: Meet the denied (top, Walter Karliner, Chapter 3), the detained (middle, Mary Matsuda, Chapter 4), and the deported (Emma Goldman, Chapter 2)—individuals who have experienced the dark side of American immigration history. Background image: The poetry of Emma Lazarus washes over the face of the Statue of Liberty. The complete text of the poem appears on page 6.

PAGE 1: Twin sisters Ines and Renate Spanier peer from a porthole of the *St. Louis* as their ship reaches Antwerp, Belgium. The girls survived the Holocaust and settled as adults in the United States.

TITLE PAGE: This fortunate family has escaped the dark side of American immigration; with feet planted firmly on Ellis Island, the parents and children await the ferry that will take them across the harbor to New York City, 1925. The less fortunate may face denied entry, detention, deportation, and other hardships.

Text copyright © 2009 Ann Bausum.
Poem "Statue of Liberty Dreams of Emma Lazarus, Awakens With Tears on Her Cheeks" copyright © 2009 Naomi Shihab Nye.
Published by the National Geographic Society. All rights reserved. Reproduction of the whole or any part of the contents without written permission form the publisher is strictly prohibited.

Library of Congress Cataloging-in-Publication Data
Bausum, Ann.
  Denied, detained, deported : stories from the dark side of American immigration / by Ann Bausum.
    p. cm.
  Includes bibliographical references and index.
  ISBN 978-1-4263-0332-6 (hardcover : alk. paper) — ISBN 978-1-4263-0333-3 (lib. bdg. : alk. paper)
  1. United States—Emigration and immigration—Government policy—History. 2. Immigrants—United States—History. I. Title.
  JV6483.B38 2009   325.73—dc22
                             2008048433

EMMA LAZARUS (1849–1887) was an American poet of Jewish-Portuguese descent. Her poem, "The New Colossus," appears on a plaque at the base of the Statue of Liberty. She was an active advocate for Jewish immigrants escaping persecution in Russia and Eastern Europe. Emma Lazarus's faith in America as a safe haven for these refugees helped shape her views on immigration.

NAOMI SHIHAB NYE (1952–) wrote "Statue of Liberty Dreams of Emma Lazarus, Awakens with Tears on Her Cheeks," as a foreword for this book. She is an award-winning poet and writer/editor of books for children and young people and a humanitarian who celebrates the power of words and uses them to bring people together. Her views on immigration were shaped in part by her Palestinian father's immigrant experience after he became a refugee in 1948. In America, his adopted land of possibility, he planted fig trees and dreamed of home. He lamented the diminishing opportunities of immigrants who followed in his footsteps.

A NOTE ON THE DESIGN: The text for the book is set in Minion Pro. The display type is Akzidenz Grotesk, and the raised quotes appear in Trajan Pro. The pictures have been colorized in a duotone combination of gold and sepia. The half sunburst evoking the Statue of Liberty's crown is a recurring ray of hope behind the chapter numbers and folios and above each raised quote.

Book design by Bea Jackson and Marty Ittner

Printed in the United States of America

CONTENTS

THE NEW COLOSSUS

Not like the brazen giant of Greek fame,
With conquering limbs astride from land to land;
Here at our sea-washed, sunset gates shall stand
A mighty woman with a torch, whose flame
Is the imprisoned lightning, and her name
Mother of Exiles. From her beacon-hand
Glows world-wide welcome; her mild eyes command
The air-bridged harbor that twin cities frame,
"Keep, ancient lands, your storied pomp!" cries she
With silent lips. "Give me your tired, your poor,
Your huddled masses yearning to breathe free,
The wretched refuse of your teeming shore,
Send these, the homeless, tempest-tost to me,
I lift my lamp beside the golden door!"

by Emma Lazarus, New York City, 1883

STATUE OF LIBERTY DREAMS OF EMMA LAZARUS, AWAKENS WITH TEARS ON HER CHEEKS

Give me your tired, your poor…
But not too tired, not too poor.
And we will give you the red tape,
the long line, white bread in its wrapper,
forms to fill out, and the looks, the stares
that say you are not where or what you should be,
not quite, not yet, you will never live up to
us.

Your huddled masses yearning to be free…
Can keep huddling. Even here. Sorry to say this.
Neighborhoods with poor drainage
Potholes, stunning gunshots…
You'll teem here too.

You dreamed a kinder place, a tree
no one would cut, a cabinet to store your clothes.
Simple jobs bringing payment on time.
Someone to stand up for you.
The way I used to do, for everyone. Holding my torch
to get you to your new home in this country stitched
of immigrants from the get-go…
But you would always be homesick. No one said that.

I was the doorkeeper, concierge, welcome chief,
But rules have changed and I'm bouncer at the big club.
Had no say in it, hear me? Any chance I could be, again,
the one I used to be?

I lift my lamp beside the golden door.
It's still up high. At night I tuck it into my robe.
And worry. What will happen to you?
Every taunt, every turn-around,
hand it over. That's not what you came here for.
I'll fold it into my rubbing rag.
Bring back a shine.

by Naomi Shihab Nye, San Antonio, 2008

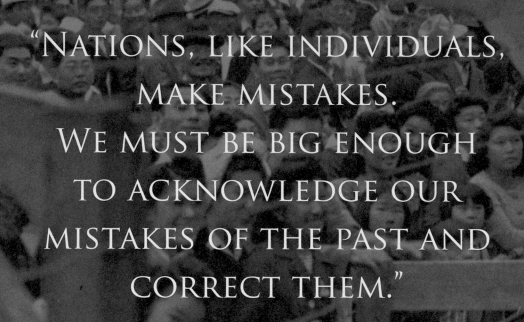

"NATIONS, LIKE INDIVIDUALS,
MAKE MISTAKES.
WE MUST BE BIG ENOUGH
TO ACKNOWLEDGE OUR
MISTAKES OF THE PAST AND
CORRECT THEM."

PRESIDENT FRANKLIN D. ROOSEVELT, MESSAGE TO CONGRESS
URGING THE REPEAL OF THE CHINESE EXCLUSION ACT, 1943

Although President Franklin D. Roosevelt
worked in 1943 to undo the wrongs of the
Chinese Exclusion Act, just the previous
year he had approved a new injustice—
the wartime imprisonment of Japanese
Americans. Background image: Inmates at
an assembly center in Southern California
watch other Japanese Americans depart by
train, bound for permanent prison camps.

INTRODUCTION

"I lift my lamp beside the golden door," proclaimed the Statue of Liberty in 1883 with the help of poet Emma Lazarus. At that time ocean liners filled with "tempest-tost" immigrants steamed eagerly toward the copper-clad symbol of fresh beginnings. Millions of newcomers fanned out across America and put down roots in the land of opportunity. The Statue's torch of "world-wide welcome" burned brightly.

Through the years, though, varying circumstances have dimmed the glow of that welcome from time to time. Those grimmer stories tend to be crowded out of history books by more plentiful tales with happier endings. This book looks the dark side of American immigration in the eye, starting with the poetic foreword written by Naomi Shihab Nye. The "rules have changed," she imagines the statue saying in the 21st century, "and I'm bouncer at the big club" now. Her statue speaks for the immigrants whose stories unfold in the pages that follow.

Meet Herbert Karliner and his family, Jews who fled Germany on the eve of World War II, sailing on the *St. Louis* in search of refuge in the new world. They became some of the hundreds of immigrants denied a safe haven from Nazi persecution.

Meet Family #19788—the Matsudas—Japanese Americans who found themselves under suspicion because they shared the same heritage as a hostile nation. They were among the thousands of first- and second-generation immigrants detained in isolated camps, regardless of their citizenship, during World War II.

Meet Emma Goldman and Alexander Berkman, Russian immigrants who tested the American commitment to free speech and discovered there are limits to American tolerance. They were but two of the hundreds of immigrants deported with haste during the period of national insecurity that followed World War I.

Denied, detained, deported. These stories represent the dark side of U.S. immigration history. They aren't just isolated goofs of public policy, random mistakes made once and never repeated. They range from the deliberate exclusion of Chinese emigrants during the 19th century to the exploitation of Mexican workers during the 20th century. And they echo through the nation's history right up to the present day.

This book examines five instances of immigration policy gone wrong. Readers may explore these individual nonfiction short stories one by one or as a chronological whole. Together they offer counterweight to the larger and better-known narrative of our nation's more positive immigration history. The opening and closing chapters of the book illustrate long-term trends of injustice. They bookend the three core stories of the book's title; these chapters put a human face on the consequences of harsh immigration decisions.

Readers will discover that forces as diverse as economics, racism, national security, and patriotism have shaped immigration history. They continue to influence policies today.

OUR GODDESS OF LIBERTY.
WHAT IS SHE TO BE? TO WHAT COMPLEXION ARE WE TO COME AT LAST?

"To what complexion are we to come at last?" warned this 1870 illustration. Immigrants and other diversity seemed to threaten the purity of the nation's image.

Well-spoken voices compete to determine how much border security the nation needs, whether to let immigrants be joined by their relatives, what obligations the country owes to newcomers, and whether illegal immigrants deserve any rights at all.

Perhaps the best way to understand current events is to look back in time. Arguments for and against immigration tend to repeat in cycles. By studying the past, we may be better able to judge when immigration policy is wise instead of short-sighted, humane instead of cruel, beneficial instead of harmful. By remembering—and learning from—yesterday's mistakes, we may avoid creating tragic history tomorrow.

"WIDE OPEN AND UNGUARDED
STAND OUR GATES,
AND THROUGH THEM PASSES
A WILD MOTLEY THRONG."

THOMAS BAILEY ALDRICH,
VERSE PUBLISHED IN THE *ATLANTIC MONTHLY*, 1882

The children of immigrants inherit a
world of prejudice beyond their making
(above, Chinese-American child in
San Francisco, 1921). Background
image: Flags flutter over the streets of
New York City's Chinatown, 1913.

EXCLUDED
"Unguarded Stand Our Gates"

IN 1882 SOMETHING CHANGED IN THE UNITED STATES, the nation of immigrants. That year, for the first time in the country's history, lawmakers voted to keep out certain newcomers. It wasn't a new idea. Benjamin Franklin had objected the previous century to the many Germans moving into Pennsylvania; they threatened to "be so numerous as to Germanize us instead of us Anglifying them," he warned in 1751. About 50 years later President John Adams and Congress threatened to deport seemingly dangerous immigrants when the fear of war prompted passage of the Alien and Sedition Acts. And, in the 1850s, more than a million Protestants joined the anti-Catholic "Know Nothing" party at a time when only six million citizens even had the right to vote.

The fear of difference in others has continued to cycle through the nation's history ever since through the voices of nativists, those citizens who dislike immigrants and oppose immigration. Rarely has the anxiety over aliens run as high or the hatred burrowed as deeply as it did in the years leading up to the legislation of 1882. Why? The nation's anti-immigration voices grew stronger because nativists had found a new common enemy: the Chinese.

As with all immigrants, two forces—push and pull—led the Chinese to leave home. Overcrowding, especially in Guangdong (Canton) Province of China, helped push residents abroad. Stories of the California gold rush of 1849 helped pull them to a place they named with two Chinese characters: Gold Mountain. For more than a century nearly all of the Chinese who immigrated to the United States were pulled from this Chinese region to the Gold Mountain State of California.

In the case of these Chinese, as with other groups of American newcomers, most of the earliest immigrants were male. They worked in mines, joined the railroad construction boom of the 1860s, and toiled at the cultivating and harvesting of crops. In short, they filled the sweatiest jobs at the bottom of the workforce, just as the Irish did who came before them, and the Eastern Europeans and Mexicans would do later on. For all these groups, even the lowliest work in the U.S. topped the opportunities of their home countries. Such jobs provided resources that could be shared with family members left behind, as well. Chinatowns and other ethnic neighborhoods grew up with these

This 1878 illustration suggested why Chinese immigrants "can live on 40 cents a day" and an American-born laborer cannot by exaggerating the difference between the lifestyle of immigrants (portrayed as eating rats, for example) and the traditional American family man.

immigrant groups, and new job opportunities developed there, too, for grocers, cooks, landlords, laundry washers, and so on.

By 1869 about 60,000 Chinese lived in the United States. That year as many as 10,000 found themselves out of work when a golden spike joined up the nation's first coast-to-coast rail line. Most returned to Chinatown in San Francisco where they found increased racism in an overcrowded labor market. Whites looked down on the Chinese as inferior. And, in an era before standardized wages, white workers resented losing jobs to Chinese willing to work for less money. Tensions grew not only in San Francisco but in other Western regions

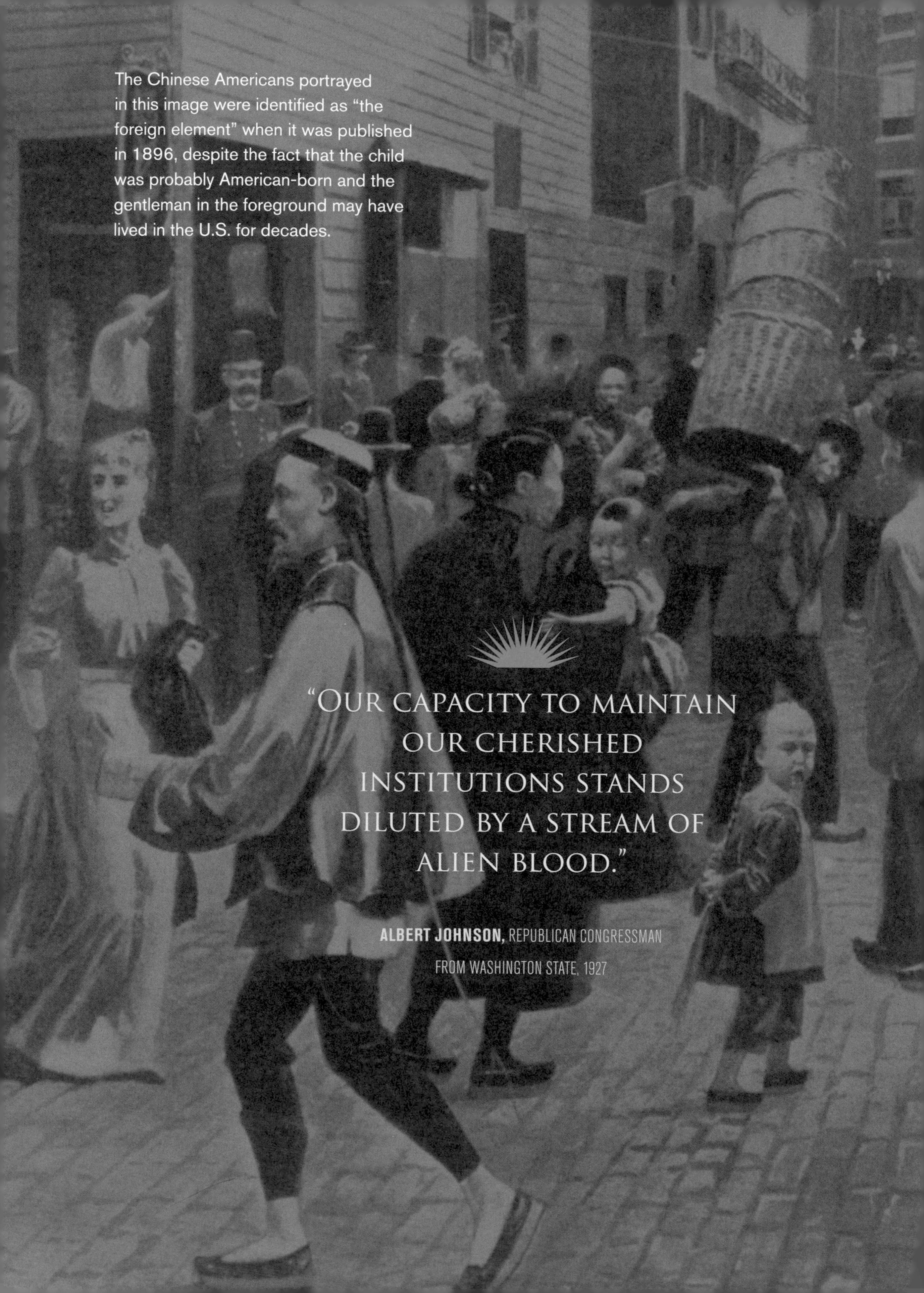

The Chinese Americans portrayed
in this image were identified as "the
foreign element" when it was published
in 1896, despite the fact that the child
was probably American-born and the
gentleman in the foreground may have
lived in the U.S. for decades.

"OUR CAPACITY TO MAINTAIN
OUR CHERISHED
INSTITUTIONS STANDS
DILUTED BY A STREAM OF
ALIEN BLOOD."

ALBERT JOHNSON, REPUBLICAN CONGRESSMAN
FROM WASHINGTON STATE, 1927

where Chinese had settled. Soon whites began to speak of the "yellow peril" that threatened to overrun the descendants of the early British colonists. The Chinese represented nothing less than an invasion of "armed men marshaled for civil war," warned one writer in 1869.

Federal politicians responded to the public's growing nativist concern by debating whether or not Asians deserved citizenship—and the voting rights that came with it. Charles Sumner, Republican Senator from Massachusetts, opposed restriction. "The greatest peril to this republic is from disloyalty to its great ideals," he advised. The so-called yellow peril existed only "in imagination; it is illusion, not a reality," he said. The majority thought otherwise, and Congress passed the Naturalization Act of 1870. Only "white persons and persons of African descent" could become citizens.

Chinese immigrants remained ineligible for citizenship until 1943 when pro-Chinese sentiments during World War II prompted a change in the law. Immigrants from other Asian countries, such as Japan, waited as many as another nine years for the full ban to be lifted. During this period, children born to aliens were among those granted citizenship by the 14th Amendment. This 1868 change to the U.S. Constitution guaranteed citizenship to "all persons born or naturalized in the United States."

Anti-Chinese sentiments grew during the years prior to the passage of the Chinese Exclusion Act of 1882. This act, with a few exceptions, ended immigration to the United States from China. The volume of

Chinese entering the U.S. dropped dramatically, and the overall number of Chinese in the country gradually declined. This law, too, was repealed in 1943, a half-century after the initial restriction. In 1882, however, nativist forces—especially organized white laborers—cheered the new law. The main opponents to restriction had been business owners and commercial farmers who liked the plentiful, inexpensive labor offered by the Chinese. Missionaries and some other religious leaders came to the defense of the Chinese, too. The news media played up the conflict and repeated the anti-Chinese message until it became accepted by others. Politicians, by and large, followed the numbers; they sided with the group with the greatest number of voters.

The Chinese Exclusion Act not only limited the growth of the Chinese American community through immigration; it limited it through reproduction, too. Chinese immigration was so new that few women had followed the early pioneers from Asia to the Gold Mountain and beyond. The Exclusion Act prevented entry of the wave of female immigrants who would otherwise have joined their fathers, brothers, and husbands in America. Even the option of visiting family and friends stranded in China died in 1888. That year Congress passed a law prohibiting re-entry to immigrants who traveled beyond the U.S. Even Chinese who happened to be abroad at the time lost the right to return to America.

Some whites—especially those who competed for jobs with the Chinese—weren't satisfied with the restrictions of the 1882 act, and

Some nativists weren't satisfied with restricting the entry of Chinese immigrants through the Exclusion Act of 1882; they wanted those Chinese Americans already in the U.S. to leave, too, at gunpoint if necessary. More than 70 anti-Chinese hate crimes took place during the mid-1880s. *Puck* portrayed the violence on an 1886 magazine cover.

sent their own message to the Chinese community: Get out of town. From such states and territories as Arizona, California, Colorado, Idaho, Kansas, Montana, Oregon, Texas, Washington, and Wyoming, whites organized boycotts of Chinese businesses, established local laws to harass them, and destroyed Chinese-owned property with hopes that the unwanted Asians would move away.

One ordinance in San Francisco taxed laundries based on how many delivery horses the establishments owned; laundries with no

"The presence in our country of Chinese laborers…should be prevented," asserted an early labor union in 1870. Resentment of Chinese immigrants by American-born workers led to acts of violence at Rock Springs, Wyoming (above, an 1885 massacre), and elsewhere.

horses (like most Chinese establishments) were taxed at more than seven times the rate of a business that used a single delivery horse. Other regions passed laws that required prospectors to be citizens, thus driving Chinese out of the mining industry. Some of the local laws failed to stand up in court and were overturned, but others—such as the segregation of Chinese students in separate non-white schools— persisted widely until well into the 20th century.

Then there were the vigilante whites who rounded up local Chinese and escorted them out of town, often at gunpoint. Such expulsions did not always proceed without bloodshed. In the Wyoming community of Rock Springs, white employees of the Union Pacific Railroad opened fire on competing Chinese workers as they drove them from town. Twenty-eight Chinese were killed and 15 wounded during the 1885 attack. The community's Chinatown became an instant ghost town, emptied of its 600-some inhabitants and mostly burned to the ground. The local newspaper applauded: "Let the demand go up from one end of the Union Pacific to the other, THE CHINESE MUST GO." Law enforcement failed to produce any witnesses to "a single criminal act committed by any known white person that day," so no one was charged with the murders. The railroad company did fire 45 of its white employees, perhaps suspecting their guilt—or perhaps to prevent them from driving off other cheap labor in the future.

Two years later 31 Chinese miners lost their lives in another racially-based hate crime. Three whites stood accused of having robbed, murdered, and mutilated the bodies of the Asian miners in an Oregon canyon, but all were cleared of the charges during their trial. "I guess if they had killed 31 white men something would have been done about it," a local rancher is reported to have observed. "None of the jury knew the Chinamen or knew much about it," he added, "so they turned the men loose."

The nation's anti-Chinese bias was so strong that Wu Ting-fang, serving in the U.S. as Chinese foreign minister, was left to ask news

Asians arriving at the West Coast of the United States found a less hospitable welcome at Angel Island in the San Francisco Bay than immigrants who reached the East Coast via Ellis Island. The California immigration center opened in 1910 and served to impede the flow of newcomers more than to encourage it.

reporters in 1901: "Why can't you be fair? Would you talk like that if mine was not a weak nation? Would you say it if the Chinese had votes?" By this time a new phrase had entered into common use in English speech: "a Chinaman's chance." Someone with a Chinaman's chance was someone with no chance at all.

It has been said that history has a way of repeating itself. Old mistakes may return in new forms when periods filled with prejudice, economic hard times, and fears about national security overtake eras of greater prosperity and confidence. Substitute Latino for Chinese, substitute

2008 for 1908, and old cries echo through current events. Calls for deportations. Fears of an alien invasion. Resentment over the sharing of resources that may be scarce. Demands for tougher laws. Somewhere in the storm, as the debate rages between nativists and non-nativists, the voice of immigrants is trying to be heard. In the words of Chinese Minister Wu Ting-fang: "Why can't you be fair?"

"I MYSELF FEEL SO CAST OUT... AND NOWHERE AT HOME."

EMMA GOLDMAN,
WRITING TO A FRIEND AFTER HER 1919 DEPORTATION

Emma Goldman and Alexander
Berkman wear deportation numbers
on Ellis Island, December 1919.
"We were photographed, finger-printed,
and tabulated like convicted criminals,"
observed Goldman. Background image:
The *Buford* carried them back to Europe.

DEPORTED
"Nowhere at Home"

FOR MILLIONS OF IMMIGRANTS, SETTING FOOT ON U.S. SOIL at Ellis Island became the first step toward fulfilling the American dream of prosperity, freedom, and happiness. Not so for the 246 men and three women held against their will at the island's detention facility on December 20, 1919. Like it or not, they would take their last step on American soil here, on this island of so many beginnings. Their one-way ticket to the land of opportunity was about to become a return voyage to a motherland they had bade farewell to as many as three decades before. Never mind the homes, friends and family, jobs, and memories they would leave behind in the U.S. They had to go. Such is the fate of the deported.

For deportee Emma Goldman, age 50, the search for the American dream had become a study of the American illusion. The daughter of poor Russian Jews, she had emigrated to the U.S. in 1885 at age 16, optimistic about moving away from oppressive czars to a land of promise and hope. After settling near family in Rochester, N.Y., however, she encountered more disappointment than reward. Her work as a seamstress in a sweatshop came with long hours and little pay. Her marriage to another immigrant left her dissatisfied and did not last. Her relations with her parents grew strained over her independence and failed marriage. Nothing seemed to fall into place for young Emma Goldman. Then current events took over her life.

Goldman was horrified when four radical labor leaders, convicted unjustly of causing a bloody riot in Chicago's Haymarket Square, were executed during November of 1887. The teenager saw shades of her own unhappiness and hardship in the treatment of these workers, and she became curious about their belief in anarchy, the absence of rule by organized government. Goldman left her family, moved to New York City, and made friends with local immigrants and anarchists. Among her first acquaintances was Alexander Berkman, another Russian newcomer stirred by the Haymarket executions. The collaborations of this pair over the next 30 years would lead both of them to fame, infamy, and, finally, deportation from the dock of Ellis Island.

Throughout those decades, Goldman, Berkman, and their associates presented anarchy as an alternative to the authority-style rule of a

Immigrants were outspoken in calls for better wages and working conditions during an era when they supplied much of the nation's labor (right, Russians march during 1909 in New York City). Background image: A bilingual flyer promotes the May 1886 rally in Chicago's Haymarket Square. "Good speakers will be present to denounce the latest atrocious act of the police, the shooting of our fellow-workmen yesterday afternoon."

typical government. They asked: Why concentrate so much power in the hands of a few people? Why not empower the individual instead? Wouldn't it be better for people to take responsibility for themselves instead of being ruled by distant authorities?

The anarchists' commitment to change echoed with a tone reminiscent of the nation's revolutionary founding fathers, and their ideas appealed to many immigrant workers. Often as not, these newcomers found themselves on the outside of the American dream, working long, hard hours for low wages while someone else reaped the

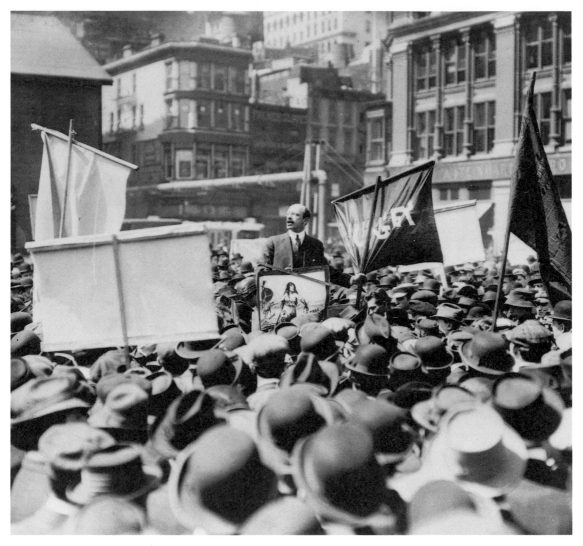

Alexander Berkman remained a fiery speaker (above, a 1914 rally in New York City's Union Square) even after spending three years in solitary confinement while in prison.

profits of their labors. Anarchists urged workers to join labor unions and go on strike, even in the face of harsh retaliation by factory owners and government authorities. One such fight at a steel mill in Homestead, Pennsylvania, during 1892 not only left strikers injured and dead. It landed Berkman in jail after he tried to assassinate a prominent executive at the plant.

Anarchists varied in their support for such acts of violence. Some saw justification in this extreme behavior; many, including Emma Goldman, did not. Later in life, Berkman tried to downplay the link between anarchy and violence. "Anarchists have no monopoly of political violence," he wrote. "The truth is that in every country, in every social movement violence has been a part of the struggle." His explanation did little to erase the tainted meaning attached to anarchy that persists to this day.

Berkman's 14-year imprisonment failed to silence Emma Goldman, though. She spoke out in support of labor unions, workers' rights, women's rights, and access to information about birth control. Her forceful confidence attracted crowds and fame during an era when few women dared to be so bold. Two prison sentences of her own—a year-long stint for urging protest among the unemployed and a briefer one for distributing birth control leaflets—failed to discourage her from public speaking.

Goldman shrugged off critical press coverage, too. News reporters labeled her the Anarchist Queen. (Berkman, released from prison in 1906, became the Anarchist King.) Eventually Goldman earned her most enduring nickname, Red Emma, because of her sympathy with the red-flag-waving revolutionaries of 20th-century Russia.

When an unknown anarchist named Leon Czolgosz mortally wounded President William McKinley in September of 1901, Goldman found herself under suspicion, too. Although Czolgosz credited her with inspiring his attack, authorities concluded that he had acted alone. His crime, even though more madness than strategy, solidified the perception of anarchists as violent.

Goldman and Berkman crossed a line that set their course toward deportation when, as the U.S. joined the fight of World War I, they encouraged Americans to avoid being drafted into forced military service. The two argued that such a requirement ran contrary to the guidelines of the U.S. Constitution and to human nature. "We will fight for what we choose to fight for," they wrote. "We will never fight simply because we are ordered to fight." Authorities disagreed. Their plans for war became more important than the anarchists' rights to protest against it. During the spring of 1917 police arrested Goldman and Berkman, charging them with conspiring to violate the Selective Service Act that ordered men to register for military service. Although they lacked the proper warrants, officers confiscated their records, not just to prosecute the pair of anarchists but to identify other supporters of their work.

By early July, the pair had been convicted unanimously in a jury trial, fined $10,000 apiece, and sentenced to two years in federal prison. Goldman and Berkman appealed to the Supreme Court, arguing that the Selective Service Act was unconstitutional, but they lost their case. On top of that blow, their judge, Julius Mayer, recommended that they be evaluated for deportation following their prison terms. "For such

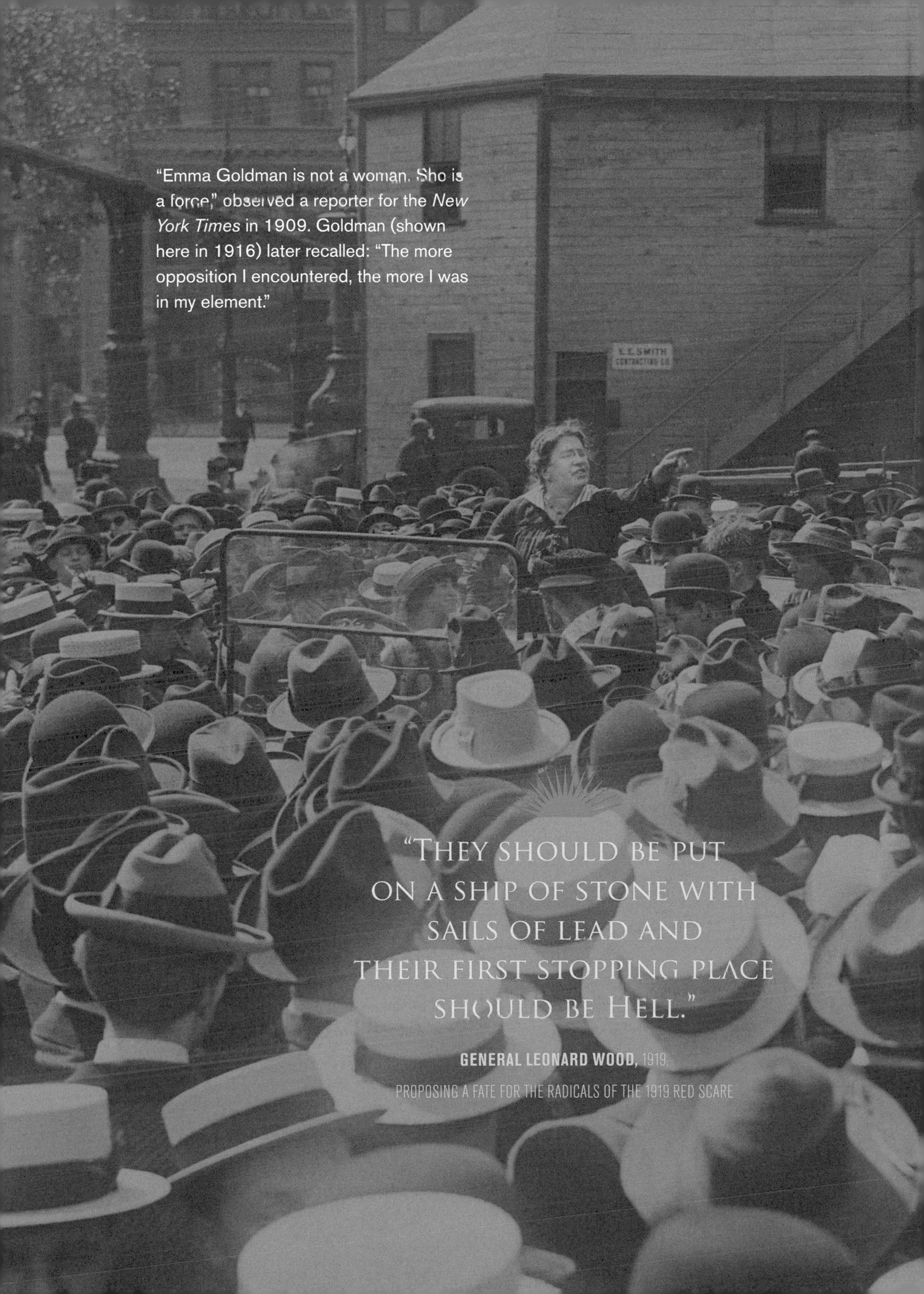

"Emma Goldman is not a woman. She is a force," observed a reporter for the *New York Times* in 1909. Goldman (shown here in 1916) later recalled: "The more opposition I encountered, the more I was in my element."

"THEY SHOULD BE PUT ON A SHIP OF STONE WITH SAILS OF LEAD AND THEIR FIRST STOPPING PLACE SHOULD BE HELL."

GENERAL LEONARD WOOD, 1919, PROPOSING A FATE FOR THE RADICALS OF THE 1919 RED SCARE

J. Edgar Hoover (left, in 1924) vowed to return "two notorious characters [Emma Goldman and Alexander Berkman] back to the colder climate of Russia where their 'Red' activities may add an element of heat to that somewhat unsettled country."

people as these, who would destroy our Government and nullify its laws, we have no place in our country," he stated.

During the early months of 1919, while Goldman and Berkman remained behind bars, a series of bombings and bomb scares fueled fears that the recent communist revolution in Russia might spread to the immigrant community in the United States. The Department of Justice responded by opening a special office within its small Bureau of Investigation. J. Edgar Hoover, a 24-year-old go-getter, took charge of this new Radical Division. His staff mounted investigations of anarchists, communists, and other agitators, including Goldman and Berkman. They planted informants among suspected troublemakers, spied on prison mail sent to and from the Anarchist King and Queen, and shadowed radical political rallies. They built their case for the deportation of Goldman and Berkman, too.

Berkman, as an alien without the rights of citizenship, fell easily within the deportation provisions of the recently passed Alien Immigration Act. The case against Goldman hinged on disproving her claim to citizenship through her brief marriage to a naturalized citizen. Investigators assembled evidence that her husband had been too young when he obtained his own citizenship. If his citizenship was invalid, so was hers.

In addition to its legal case, Hoover's unit stirred up public support for the deportation of Goldman, Berkman, and other radicals. They sent ominous reports to the newspapers, disclosed alarming tidbits of intelligence to lawmakers, and emphasized the need for expanded watchfulness. They suggested that radical immigrants posed a security threat to the United States, a so-called red menace (named for the signature color of the communist fight in Russia). Their public relations campaign set in motion what became known as the Red Scare. The size and effects of the scare quickly grew far beyond the legitimate concerns that lay at its foundation.

Analysis by historians of newly declassified documents suggests that an interest in more than national security helped fuel the scare. The Red Scare provided a convenient justification for expanding the Bureau of Investigation at a time when others were calling for the office to shrink. The size of Hoover's Radical Division, including its funding and staff, grew with the mounting fears, for example. Politicians exploited fears over the red menace, too. Potential candidates for the next year's presidential election tied their names to the cause of keeping Americans safe from anarchists and other radicals. Both political parties played this game, egged on by Republicans who had painted Democrats during 1918 elections as favoring immigrants and radicals over patriots.

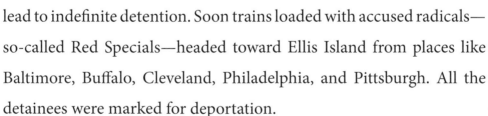

On November 7, 1919, the Bureau of Investigation executed simultaneous raids in over a dozen U.S. cities and arrested more than 1,000 suspected radicals. These dramatic, high-profile actions were dubbed the Palmer raids, named for A. Mitchell Palmer, a presidential hopeful who headed the Justice Department. Many suspects found themselves apprehended without arrest warrants, detained without access to legal counsel, and subjected to physical abuse during questioning. A coerced confession of labor union membership might lead to indefinite detention. Soon trains loaded with accused radicals— so-called Red Specials—headed toward Ellis Island from places like Baltimore, Buffalo, Cleveland, Philadelphia, and Pittsburgh. All the detainees were marked for deportation.

At the same time, deportation hearings proceeded against Goldman and Berkman, whose prison terms had ended in late September. Their attorney condemned "the present hysteria" and argued that the government had an obligation to offer "justice to even the most unpopular citizen or

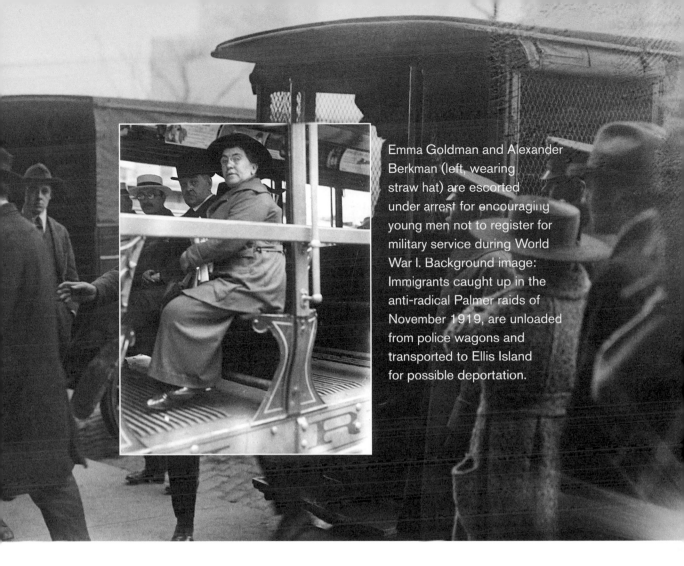

Emma Goldman and Alexander Berkman (left, wearing straw hat) are escorted under arrest for encouraging young men not to register for military service during World War I. Background image: Immigrants caught up in the anti-radical Palmer raids of November 1919, are unloaded from police wagons and transported to Ellis Island for possible deportation.

alien holding the most unpopular views at the most unpopular time." In contrast, Hoover had recently described the pair as "beyond doubt, two of the most dangerous anarchists in this country and [granting them permission] to return to the community will result in undue harm." Authorities sided with Hoover and ordered the pair of radicals to report to Ellis Island by December 5. Deportation would follow.

From their detention cells, Goldman and Berkman authored a 32-page pamphlet called "Deportation: Its Meaning and Menace." They argued that their deportations were the result of politics, not national security. Among other motives, they charged that government and business leaders hoped the crackdown on radicals would undermine efforts to establish labor unions and the fight for worker rights. They concluded their booklet by quoting famous people who would, "if still alive and of foreign birth, not be permitted on American shores if they tried to land here, or, if born Americans, they would be threatened by deportation" for expressing such radical thoughts. Among those quoted were the poet Ralph Waldo Emerson and Presidents Abraham Lincoln and Thomas Jefferson.

The pair of confined anarchists watched the number of their companions swell. Most of the 249 aliens who eventually arrived had earned their deportation orders by belonging to the recently outlawed Union of Russian Workers. About a dozen had entered the country illegally or broken general laws. The rest, 51 of them including Goldman and Berkman, were being deported as alien anarchists. All but three of them were male.

The deportees lived under guard, segregated by gender, and uncertain of their date of deportation, or even their destination. Most of the detainees were originally from Russia and expected to be returned there, but no one would confirm the plans. A wire screen separated the inmates from all visitors. There would be no farewell hugs between husbands and wives or fathers and children. Mail passed through censors at a snail's pace, adding to the sense of isolation on the island.

Then, during the early, frozen hours of December 21, guards awoke the detainees and hustled them outside. They marched the inmates single file between two rows of federal officers, ushered them aboard a small boat, and transferred them in New York harbor onto the *Buford*, a large old military troop transport ship. J. Edgar Hoover was among the government officials who attended the send off. No one notified family members, and no friends were present. By dawn the prisoners were headed out to sea on what newspapers nicknamed the "Red Ark." An armed crew, reinforced by some 200 U.S. soldiers, manned the vessel.

Officials boasted that more Red Arks would sail soon. But, even as the *Buford* lumbered for 26 days across the Atlantic, the momentum of the Red Scare began to die. By the time the banished travelers had reached their final destination—Russia, as predicted—the Red Scare was fading in the United States. Louis Post, serving as acting Secretary of Labor during 1920, deserves partial credit for the change. He insisted that procedures take precedence over hysteria and that all immigration laws overseen by his department be followed diligently. Prominent lawyers helped, too. They accused the Justice Department of conducting "utterly illegal acts." The raids and deportations "have caused widespread suffering and unrest, have struck at the foundation of American free institutions, and have brought the name of our country to disgrace," they charged.

The halt of the Red Scare may have seemed like a victory for advocates of social justice, but it was not a defeat for the forces that had promoted it, either. With or without deportations, the bullying tactics of the Radical Division had the effect of muting the voice of the radical labor movement. So did the increased restrictions on alien entry and rights. Immigrants were on notice: stay in your place or risk consequences. Even radical thought became easier to discredit as dangerous and un-American.

A second Red Scare emerged with the ending of the next World War in 1945, for example. This time communism, not anarchy, became the perceived threat. Many of the same tactics and arguments from the first Red Scare appeared again. They included illegal surveillance, interrogations, the exploitation of public fears, the jailing of suspected communists, and a new round of deportations. Some of the same figures and forces were even involved. By this time, for example, the small Justice Department Bureau of Investigation had grown into the powerful Federal Bureau of Investigation, or FBI, headed by none other than J. Edgar Hoover.

A variation of the Red Scare—directed at Islamic extremists—followed the 9-11 terrorist attacks of 2001. As with earlier episodes, kernels of genuine danger became lost in political maneuvers, misconduct, and debate. What rights do the accused have to the traditional protections of access to lawyers, family, and trial? Do these

Emma Goldman returned to the United States for an extended visit in 1934 at the age of 64. Spark and challenge endured in the fiery speaker who had been branded "the yellow-haired evangel of disorder" during her youth.

The brief love affair that united Emma Goldman and Alexander Berkman when they met in 1889 soon mellowed into a collaborative friendship that would last for the rest of their lives. They affectionately called one another Sasha (Berkman's nickname) and "my sailor" (Goldman's); the friends lived nearby one another for much of their adult lives (left, in France, 1935). Background image: Memorial to the executed Haymarket Square anarchists, Waldheim Cemetery, Chicago.

rights vary for U.S. citizens versus the citizens of other countries? What individual rights should be sacrificed in the name of homeland security? Can the country honor its commitment to freedom and democracy when it compromises those founding principles? As in past scares, conflicting answers to such questions will persist until the dangers are passed.

Emma Goldman and Alexander Berkman lived in Russia for fewer than two years. The ideals of the Russian Revolution had proved difficult to put into practice, they discovered, and they left their birth country for good. Berkman never returned to the United States; he died in France during 1936 at age 65. Goldman saw the U.S. only once more, in 1934, when she gained permission for a three-month-long lecture tour.

"You are still free in America," she commended during her visit. "You are free to come here and listen to me, with no army of police descending upon you. No spies enter your homes for incriminating documents. No legalized assassins shoot you down in the streets." Perhaps she spoke with a touch of irony—after all, officials had seized documents illegally from her, and police had fired on protesters in Haymarket Square. But, Goldman knew, plenty of governments behaved worse, including ones she had previously admired, such as Russia.

Following her death in 1940 at age 70, Emma Goldman made one final trip to the United States. At her request, and with the permission of U.S. authorities, her remains were laid to rest in a cemetery in Chicago. The bodies of the executed Haymarket Square anarchists rest nearby.

"WHAT STARTED AS A VOYAGE OF FREEDOM IS NOW A VOYAGE OF DOOM."

JOSEF JOSEPH, DIARY ENTRY DURING
HIS 1939 VOYAGE ON THE *ST. LOUIS*

"Everyone seems convinced they will never see Germany again," wrote Captain Gustav Schröder as his ship full of refugees set sail for North America. Among the passengers was the Karliner family (above, eldest son Walter). Background image: The *St. Louis* departs Hamburg, Germany.

DENIED
"A Voyage of Doom"

BY 1939, BEING JEWISH IN NAZI GERMANY OFTEN meant one thing: leaving home. That spring the Jewish passengers who boarded the *St. Louis* probably counted themselves among the lucky. They were escaping from the destruction of their homes, the looting of their businesses, and the limits placed on their rights by the Jew-hating dictator Adolf Hitler. They were leaving behind the country's concentration camps, too, places where some of them had already been jailed. Now a cruise across the Atlantic on a luxury liner awaited them—and the promise of finding refuge and safety in the new world.

Herb Karliner, age 12, and his three siblings were among the 937 passengers on board the *St. Louis* when she weighed anchor on May 13, 1939, bound for Cuba. All but seven of their fellow passengers were

Jewish refugees from Germany. Most of them, like the Karliner family, planned to emigrate eventually to the nearby United States. Their stay in Cuba would last only as long as it took for their immigration quota numbers to become valid for entry. Some travelers expected to wait a year or more while Germans with lower numbers took their turns entering the U.S.

As bands played and onlookers waved from the dock, Herb's parents may have gazed wistfully at the receding German horizon, perhaps wondering if they would ever see their homeland again. Herb left his native land with fewer regrets. "I was a boy who wanted to see the world," he recalled decades later.

In the years before the Karliners' departure, it had seemed that the longer Hitler stayed in power, the worse their lives became. "First [Jews] were ordered off the sidewalks," Herb remembers. "Then they banned us from the movie theaters….I liked to play soccer [but after awhile]…they tossed me off the team….No Jews allowed."

Any hopes for Herb and other German Jews that such treatment would cease were shattered on November 9, 1938, with Kristallnacht, or the "Night of Broken Glass." Nazi guards rampaged across the country to avenge the recent murder of a German official by a Jewish youth. They vandalized and looted hundreds of Jewish-owned shops and homes, arrested thousands of Jews for confinement in concentration camps, and set fire to some 200 Jewish synagogues. Scores of Jews lost their lives.

In Germany, the Karliners lived behind their family grocery store (above). The store did not reopen after Nazis ransacked it during Kristallnacht in 1938. Instead the family made plans to flee their homeland.

Herb's family awoke to find their grocery store business in a shambles. Then word came that the local synagogue was on fire. When Herb's father, Josef, tried to prevent its sacred Torah scrolls from being burned, Nazis attacked him. Later that day authorities arrested him and sent him to the concentration camp at Buchenwald. Mr. Karliner could be released, they said, if his family promised to leave Germany. This was the story that brought the Karliners to the *St. Louis*. The ship's other passengers walked on board with similar tales of horror and woe.

Now things were looking up, starting with a two-week pleasure cruise to Cuba. The refugees proceeded to stroll on the decks of the luxury liner, sample its multi-course menus, and dance to live music. Children explored the ship's nooks and crannies, splashed in a swimming pool, and played ping-pong and shuffleboard. Passengers watched movies, roller skated on the boat's wooden decks, celebrated

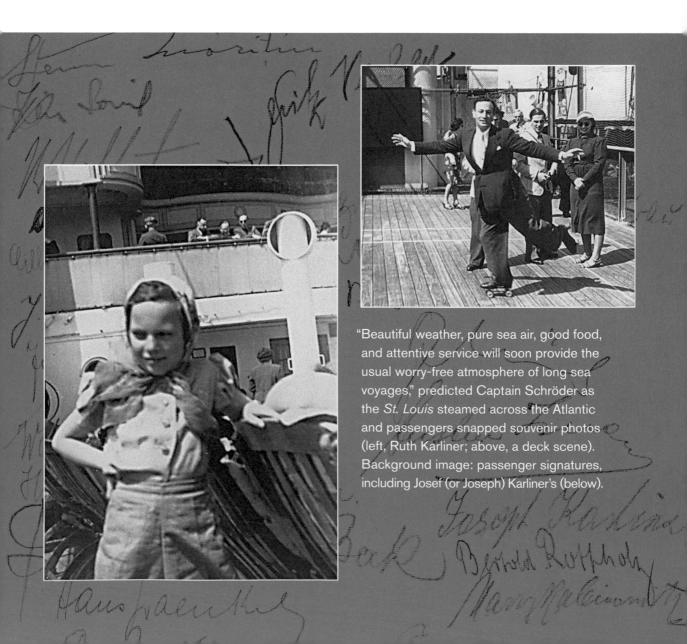

"Beautiful weather, pure sea air, good food, and attentive service will soon provide the usual worry-free atmosphere of long sea voyages," predicted Captain Schröder as the *St. Louis* steamed across the Atlantic and passengers snapped souvenir photos (left, Ruth Karliner; above, a deck scene). Background image: passenger signatures, including Josef (or Joseph) Karliner's (below).

birthdays, drank champagne, visited the on-board beauty salon, and lounged in sunny deck chairs. Only the death of an already ill passenger darkened the journey. The Nazi swastika might fly over the vessel, but every passing day took the refugees on the *St. Louis* farther from the tyranny of Adolf Hitler and closer to a fresh start in new countries.

A description of photographs taken during the voyage helps convey the scene: A smiling Herb Karliner stands next to his father, who is lounging under a blanket on a deck chair. His mother Martha visits with other grown-ups in the dining room. Ilse, the oldest child in the family at age 16, poses to have her picture made on deck with a tall teenage boy she has met during the voyage. Herb's younger sister, Ruth, at 11, stands beside a deck chair, her hair swept back under a kerchief, her attention focused on a momentary distraction. Herb and his brother Walter, age 14, pal around with groups of other children their ages.

On May 27 an early-morning blast from the ship's horn signaled the arrival of the *St. Louis* at Havana, Cuba. "The sky is dark blue, but I can make out a few white buildings stark against it," one passenger recorded immediately in her diary. "There are stars in the sky. It's like a dream." Alas, the dreamlike quality of their arrival dissolved all too quickly into a day-lit nightmare. The *St. Louis* lay at anchor, tantalizingly close to shore, but seemingly unable to reach her destination. Why didn't the ship dock and prepare for the passengers to depart? Excitement soured into unease, then worry, then despair.

The problem came down to pieces of paper. Most of the passengers had, as instructed in Germany, purchased Cuban landing permits prior to their departure. A handful had, for good measure, secured official Cuban visas, too. Few emigrants understood the finer distinctions between these documents, and none knew that just days before the *St. Louis* set sail from Europe, Cuban officials had declared the simple landing permits invalid. Even ship captain Gustav Schröder had not learned this news until after the voyage was underway.

Several factors contributed to the change of Cuban policy, including a rise in local Nazi influence and alarm over the swelling population of Jewish immigrants seeking haven there. Word that more refugee ships were steaming toward the region only added to the hasty closing of Cuba's immigration doors.

Just 28 of the ship's passengers were allowed to disembark later that day. They included six non-Jewish passengers—two Cubans and four Spaniards—as well as the 22 Jewish passengers who held Cuban visas. Those left behind faced the torture of uncertain fates. Rumors flew. Passengers debated their options. Would Cuban authorities have a change of heart and admit them? Might another country take them in? Could those with plans to emigrate to the United States gain permission to enter ahead of schedule? What if no one would take them in? Would they have to return to renewed harassment, uncertainty, and fear in Germany?

Locals yelled greetings from rented boats to their friends and relatives marooned in the Cuban harbor. They predicted landing "*mañana*," or tomorrow, "but *mañana* never came," Herbert Karliner noted.

On the third day of lying at anchor in Havana harbor, one passenger snapped. Max Loewe, husband and father, slit his wrists and jumped overboard. He was rescued and taken ashore for treatment, but passengers organized suicide watches to prevent further acts of desperation. Finally, after nearly a week of negotiation, authorities ordered the *St. Louis* to depart. Passengers wept at the news, as did many among the thousands of friends and spectators who watched from shore. More than two dozen harbor police boats shadowed the ship's departure on June 2 to assure no one else jumped overboard.

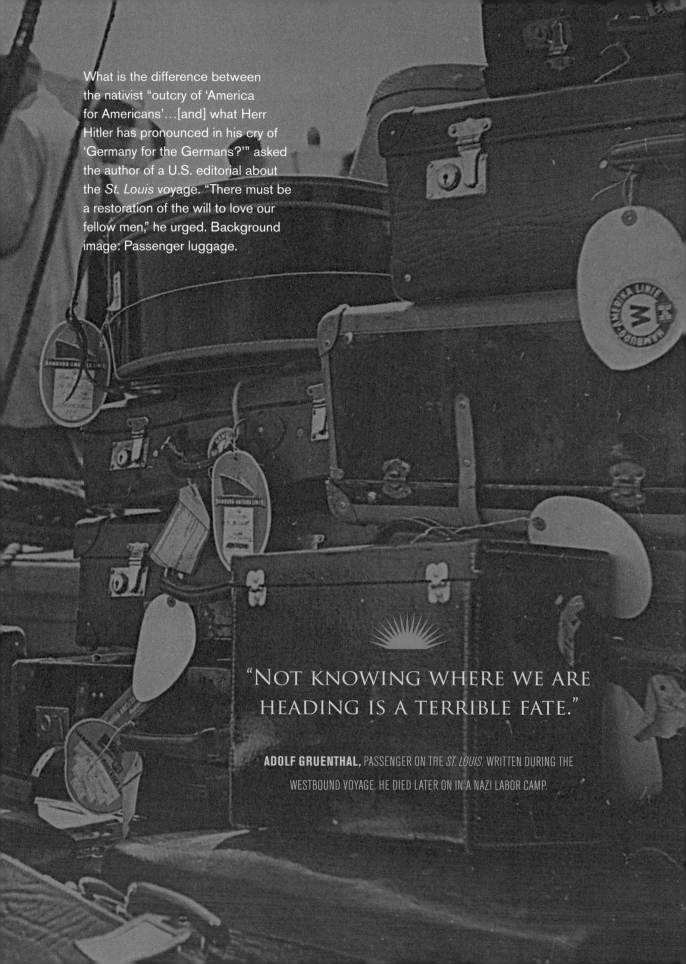

What is the difference between the nativist "outcry of 'America for Americans'…[and] what Herr Hitler has pronounced in his cry of 'Germany for the Germans?'" asked the author of a U.S. editorial about the *St. Louis* voyage. "There must be a restoration of the will to love our fellow men," he urged. Background image: Passenger luggage.

"NOT KNOWING WHERE WE ARE HEADING IS A TERRIBLE FATE."

ADOLF GRUENTHAL, PASSENGER ON THE *ST. LOUIS,* WRITTEN DURING THE WESTBOUND VOYAGE. HE DIED LATER ON IN A NAZI LABOR CAMP.

Captain Schröder headed the *St. Louis* toward the Florida coast with hopes that Americans might be more welcoming than the Cubans. The passengers shared his optimism. They sent messages to U.S. government officials, including President Franklin D. Roosevelt. The ship's children wrote appeals for help to his wife Eleanor Roosevelt. Liesel Joseph, then age 10, recalled years later how for emigrants at that time "America was a magic word. It was the be-all and end-all. We knew America would not let us down."

But the United States did let the passengers down. It did not matter that more than 700 of them held quota numbers for eventual admission to the country. It did not matter that Americans overwhelmingly disapproved of Hitler's treatment of German Jews and rejected his anti-Jewish beliefs. What did matter was that U.S. citizens felt equally strongly that immigration quotas should not be relaxed. Jobs were in short supply. Distrust of foreigners remained high. The stream of refugees seemed endless.

Many Americans felt the United States had sheltered enough refugees. President Roosevelt had extended the stays for some 15,000 Germans visiting the U.S., for example, and the United States had already taken in more refugees than any other country. Such strong public opinions left President Roosevelt little room for negotiation. He faced an uncertain reelection bid the next year, and he didn't need to alienate voters by disagreeing with their preferences.

So, as the *St. Louis* cruised near Miami—close enough for the passengers to see the city's lights at night, and for Herb Karliner to glimpse his first palm trees by day—President Roosevelt said and did nothing. With all ports seemingly closed in North America, Captain Schröder received orders to return to Germany. On June 7, the *St. Louis* turned eastward, 11 days after first reaching Havana.

The only remaining hope was that the refugees would be offered sanctuary in other European countries before the ship reached Germany. In the end, that is exactly what happened. When the ship was halfway back across the Atlantic, word reached the *St. Louis* that four European nations would take in the refugees. No one would be returned to Germany. Champagne corks flew at the news, and the gloom of recent days lifted. "The children of the *St. Louis* are most thankful to you for rescuing them out of deepest despair," Liesel Joseph wrote soon after to one of the organizers of the plan.

Five weeks to the day after boarding the ship, passengers disembarked at Antwerp, Belgium. Two hundred fourteen of the refugees remained in Belgium, 224 prepared to travel to France (including the Karliner family), 287 boarded a new ship headed for the United Kingdom, and 181 traveled to the nearby Netherlands. After Max Loewe recovered from his suicide attempt, he would join his family in England. The only remaining non-Jewish passenger, a Hungarian, returned to his home.

Seemingly the voyage of the *St. Louis* had come to a happy conclusion. It hadn't been an easy voyage. It hadn't made a lot of sense. But it had ended with everyone finding shelter away from Hitler's dictatorship. Alas, this resolution was short lived. Within months Adolf Hitler invaded Poland, and Europe began to slip into the Second World War. Soon, of the four sheltering nations, only the United Kingdom remained free of Nazi reach. More than half of the former *St. Louis* passengers were back in harm's way.

Belgian officials await the docking of the *St. Louis* at Antwerp. The German ship's crew members, assembled on deck, raise their arms in the Nazi salute during the arrival.

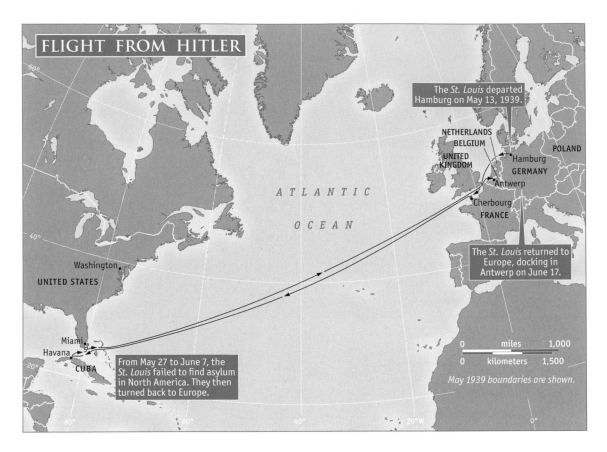

FLIGHT FROM HITLER

The *St. Louis* departed Hamburg on May 13, 1939.

The *St. Louis* returned to Europe, docking in Antwerp on June 17.

From May 27 to June 7, the *St. Louis* failed to find asylum in North America. They then turned back to Europe.

NETHERLANDS
BELGIUM
UNITED KINGDOM
POLAND
Hamburg
GERMANY
Antwerp
Cherbourg
FRANCE

ATLANTIC

OCEAN

Washington
UNITED STATES

Miami
Havana
CUBA

miles 1,000
kilometers 1,500
May 1939 boundaries are shown.

The *St. Louis* traveled from Germany to Belgium by way of North America. At times the captain steered his vessel in aimless circles, unsure of where he would be allowed to land.

Until recently, historians and others have assumed that most of the 619 passengers who settled on the European continent must have perished in the Nazi Holocaust—murdered, starved, or worked to death in its concentration camps. At the end of the 20th century, staff members at the United States Holocaust Memorial Museum tested that assumption. Over the course of ten years, researchers Sarah Ogilvie and Scott Miller tracked down the fates of every *St. Louis* passenger, including Herb Karliner and his family.

They learned that the Karliner family had found itself divided up after reaching France. Herb's life became a series of stays at group homes for refugee children, repeated moves to escape the advance of Nazi rule in France, an apprenticeship to a baker, the assumption of an assumed identity as a non-Jewish Frenchman, and, in the final months before Allied forces liberated the territory, a life alone on the run. By war's end, he had grown from a 12-year-old boy into an 18-year-old man.

His brother Walter experienced a similar round of shelter in assorted group homes, an apprenticeship (as a cabinet maker), and an assumed identity that protected him until the end of the war. The rest of the Karliner family was less lucky. Josef, Martha, and their daughters survived in Nazi-occupied France until 1942 when they were swept up with other known Jews for transport to concentration camps. None of the captured Karliners survived. The Karliner boys were unable to confirm the fates of their family members until the war ended in 1945.

Two years later the brothers emigrated to the U.S., admitted under the same quota system that had failed to find room for them before the war. Herb Karliner married a woman he had met in a French children's home. The couple settled in Miami, the same palm-filled city Herb had glimpsed from the decks of the *St. Louis*. Taking advantage of his wartime apprenticeship, Herb opened a bakery. Walter established an antique shop in Connecticut. Both brothers are still living.

The Holocaust Museum researchers learned that the Karliners' story mirrored the fates of other *St. Louis* passengers—separation, heroic survival, wrenching loss, quirks of fate and chance. Their study revealed that many more passengers from the *St. Louis* had survived than had previously been thought, too. Nonetheless, by their count, 254 of the ship's 930 Jewish passengers perished due to the Holocaust. The rest either survived the war in Europe or succeeded in emigrating before war engulfed the continent.

Hindsight, that look back at the past with the benefit of present knowledge, offers a harsh judgment of the U.S. refusal to shelter the *St. Louis* passengers. If only President Roosevelt or others had intervened on their behalf, the passengers would have escaped further Nazi persecution. In 1939, though, no one knew how things would turn out. No one knew that Germany would overrun so much territory, and do so that quickly. No one knew, either, that Hitler would change his treatment of the Jews from a policy of forced exile into one of mass captivity and murder. It seemed reasonable to assume at the time that the *St. Louis* refugees were safe.

Only with hindsight does it appear obvious that the United States should have done more. The U.S. could have admitted several years' worth of German immigration quota numbers all at once, for example—as an administrator proposed at the time—instead of handing out numbers that could not be used for entry until a future year. And it could have

Ilse Karliner (upper photo, in
German-occupied France), sister Ruth
(lower photo with her brother Herbert), and their parents did
not escape the Nazi Holocaust. Herbert and Walter Karliner
survived the war under assumed identities in southern France.

relaxed its interpretation of existing immigration laws, making it easier
for poor and dependent refugees to qualify for entrance.

But there were no guarantees in 1939 that the United States was
beyond attack, either. Harm could have followed the refugees to the
United States. And, might intervention by Roosevelt have cost him
reelection? How would the nation have weathered the world war

"All's well that ends well," read the caption under the final photo (background image) of the Altschul family scrapbook from their *St. Louis* voyage. Their journey ended safely with refuge in Great Britain. Not so for five members of the Dublon family (right). The parents, a brother, and their two daughters all died at Auschwitz concentration camp.

Ende gut~ alles gut.

under a different, less experienced President? Hindsight raises as many questions as it answers.

Wars and the tyranny of dictatorships seem to create new waves of refugees for each generation, and the United States remains the nation of choice for many of these exiles. The end of the Vietnam War in 1975 pushed thousands of refugees to take to the open seas, for example. More than 200,000 of these so-called boat people settled eventually in the U.S. Among the waves of Cubans who have sought shelter in the U.S. during the rule of Fidel Castro, are the thousands who crowded into pleasure boats or piled onto homemade rafts in 1980 and headed for Florida. The U.S. took them in, too.

Herb Karliner, by then a long-time resident of Miami, couldn't help but feel bitter as he watched the newcomers flood his adopted state. "You know what I cannot understand?" he asked a fellow *St. Louis* survivor some years later. "We were not allowed in Cuba [or the U.S.]…and then in 1980, 125,000 Cubans were let into Florida without a question….And here we were, 900 people running away from Nazis, and we could not come."

His companion, someone with whom he had once played on the decks of the *St. Louis*, searched for hope and comfort as he formed his answer. "Herb," he said, "I like to think [that] because of us is why they let them in."

Japanese Americans of all ages were
rounded up and imprisoned in the spring
of 1942, their loyalty under suspicion
following the recent Japanese attack on
Pearl Harbor, Hawaii. Background image:
Relocation camp barracks in Colorado.

"OUR TRAIN RUMBLED
TOWARDS AN UNKNOWN
DESTINATION, CARRYING US TO
SOME PLACE, SOMEWHERE,
FOR SOME UNKNOWN LENGTH OF
TIME, AND POSSIBLY TO OUR DEATH.
UNCERTAINTY WAS ALL WE KNEW."

MARY MATSUDA GRUENEWALD, RECOLLECTING
HER FAMILY'S RELOCATION DURING 1942

DETAINED
"Uncertainty Was All We Knew"

THREE NUMBERS BEGIN THE STORY OF JAPANESE-American immigration: Ichi, ni, san. One, two, three. They identify the first three generations of Japanese-American immigrants: Issei, Nisei, Sansei. The Issei traveled from Japan around the turn of the last century to make a new home for themselves in America. Their children, the Nisei, became the first generation born in the United States with Japanese heritage. Most of their children, the Sansei, were born after World War II, so they did not live through what became a defining event in the lives of their parents and grandparents—mass imprisonment while their old and new homelands went to war.

For the Issei and Nisei, the world changed on December 7, 1941, when Japanese bombers attacked the U.S. Naval fleet stationed at Pearl Harbor, Hawaii. "It was my last carefree morning," writes Mary Matsuda Gruenewald in her memoir *Looking Like the Enemy: My*

During World War II the Matsuda family (left, in 1933) was forced to leave their home (above) and live in prison camps. "I was old enough to know that something was dreadfully wrong, but still frightened, like a lost child," Mary (far left) recalls in her memoir.

Years of Imprisonment in Japanese-American Internment Camps. Until she heard the news, she was "preoccupied with all the trivial cares and worries of a 16-year-old American teenager." After the news she shared the fears of the Japanese-American community that, because they looked like the enemy, they would be treated like the enemy.

In 1941 Mary lived with her older brother, Yoneichi, and her parents on a strawberry farm on Vashon Island, Washington. The Matsuda family story mirrored the history of other Japanese Americans. Her father had immigrated as a young man in 1898; her mother had arrived two decades later. As Asian immigrants, neither was eligible for American citizenship. Mary's parents primarily spoke and wrote in Japanese. Mary and her brother were bilingual, attending public school all week and spending Saturdays at Japanese school where they learned Japanese writing and arts. Their births on U.S. soil made them U.S. citizens.

The bombing of Pearl Harbor brought calls for the imprisonment of West Coast Japanese Americans. These demands were fueled by decades of simmering racism, anger over the death and destruction caused at Pearl Harbor, and anxieties over the potential security threat that might be posed by people who shared heritage with an enemy nation. "A Jap's a Jap….It makes no difference whether he is an American citizen," summed up Lieut. General John L. DeWitt.

On February 19, 1942, President Franklin D. Roosevelt, in response to mounting calls for action and discouraging battlefront reports, signed Executive Order 9066. The order authorized the military to remove potential enemies from West Coast states, relocate them elsewhere, and detain them indefinitely. In the end, some 120,000 Japanese Americans were imprisoned, a majority of them U.S.-born citizens. Ironically one place untouched by the order was the only place Japan had attacked—Hawaii. Japanese Americans there lived out the war in relative liberty because they provided so much of the islands' workforce.

When the Matsudas learned in early 1942 that government officials had begun searching the homes of Japanese Americans on nearby islands, they collected all of their possessions that might taint them as un-American. Then they set them on fire. They burned their ancestors' photos. They burned phonograph records of Japanese music. They burned books written in Japanese script. They burned ceremonial dolls dressed in Japanese clothing. "That fateful day we burned all of our cultural treasures in the oil-burning stove in the living room," Mary recollects sadly in her memoir.

Government officials began evicting Japanese Americans from restricted areas in March. The Matsudas, like other families, were given just seven days' notice of their evacuation date, May 16, 1942. They made arrangements for someone to manage their farm. Then they packed. Each person was allowed to bring only what could be carried in two suitcases. No exceptions. No shipping. No pets. Evacuees were expected to bring their own bed sheets, dishes, and eating utensils. No indication was provided of how long they might be gone, where they would be taken, what climate to prepare for, or if they would ever return to their homes.

Most members of the Japanese-American community saw few options other than to cooperate. Mary's father expressed the thoughts

Boxcars full of baggage accompanied Japanese Americans on their way to wartime detention camps. The evacuees (including the young boy pictured above) traveled in passenger compartments elsewhere on the train.

of many: "We'll do whatever we can to show that we are good citizens in spite of everything." The Japanese expression *"Shigata ganai"* became a common refrain. "It can't be helped." Those exposed to racial taunting and threats even welcomed the apparent safety offered by armed guards in a secured area. Only a few individuals sought to challenge the relocation and related restrictions, and those cases moved too slowly through the courts to offer any immediate halt in the evacuation.

On evacuation day the Matsudas said goodbye to their farm, their cat, and their dog, and then they hiked a mile with their luggage to an assembly area. Guards armed with guns and bayonets took charge and dispensed tags printed with a predetermined identification number, 19788. The Matsudas attached tags to all of

Relocation camps contained dozens
of blocks of housing barracks, typically
with five one-room living spaces each,
grouped around common dining and
bathing facilities. Background image:
Assembly Center, Pomona, Calif., 1942.

"WHEN THE WAR IS OVER...
WE AS AMERICANS ARE GOING
TO REGRET THE UNAVOIDABLE
INJUSTICES THAT MAY HAVE
BEEN DONE."

MILTON EISENHOWER, DIRECTOR,
WAR RELOCATION AUTHORITY APRIL 1, 1942

their suitcases. Then they each attached a tag to themselves. They had become Family Number 19788.

Onlookers spat at them and shouted as they walked off their ferry through Seattle to a waiting train. "Get outta here, you God damn Japs!" yelled one spectator. The windows of their crowded train were darkened so that they could not see where they were going. When the Matsudas stopped traveling three days later, they found themselves at Pinedale Assembly Center, one of 15 temporary facilities where evacuees lived while permanent camps were constructed. The Matsudas were among the lucky ones. Their California camp had actual barracks; many evacuees ended up at fairgrounds and racetracks where some people were literally housed in animal stalls.

The Matsuda family remained at Pinedale for about six weeks. Then the government shipped a train-load of evacuees, including Family Number 19788, to the Tule Lake Relocation Camp in northern California. (Members of the Matsuda family would eventually live at camps in Wyoming and Idaho, too.) Between May and October of 1942 all of the assembly center residents were relocated to one of ten prison camps. The camps bore romantic-sounding names like Heart Mountain and Topaz, but inmates found little to celebrate about the locations. All of the camps were in isolated, desolate areas—usually desert environments—and generally featured temperature extremes, dust storms, and hastily constructed facilities, albeit at a cost of $80 million. Smaller camps held about 7,500 people; the largest held more than 18,000.

Whatever the location, each camp resembled the next. Interior barrack walls separated the housing units only to the base of the roof line. Open space filled the triangular gap below the pitched roof and allowed sounds to travel freely from one end of the barracks to the other. Some people hung sheets or blankets to create interior "walls" within their small 20-by-20-foot living spaces. The barracks had no running water and minimal electricity and lighting. Separate bathhouses contained rows of communal shower heads and toilet stalls without doors. Residents in the housing blocks ate their meals in Army-style mess halls. The entire camp package was wrapped up with strings of barbed wire and topped with guard towers and searchlights.

A curious vocabulary arose to describe these facilities and their residents. Early references to centers as concentration camps—even by President Roosevelt—were dropped in favor of euphemisms such as assembly centers, relocation centers, and internment camps. Today they might best be termed prison camps. The dislocated were referred to as residents not as prisoners. They were being evacuated, not evicted. Their spartan living spaces were dubbed apartments, not cells.

In *Looking Like the Enemy,* Mary documents the range of emotions she experienced during her more than two years of imprisonment, ones that repeated themselves thousands of times over in the lives of other

Children worked to improvise and adapt in the harsh settings of relocation camps (above, playing games in Heart Mountain, Wyoming, 1943).

camp inmates. She struggles with the unlifting sadness of depression. She wrestles with insatiable longings for the sights, activities, and tastes of home. She experiences waves of anger that have no outlet for expression. Boredom fills her days. Nightmares haunt her sleep. Most of all, she lives scared for her safety in a world of constant surveillance and uncertainty. "My deep fear [was] that someday when I least expected it, the soldiers would come and kill us all," she admits.

Inmates coped by trying to establish a sense of familiarity and community within their prison-like environment. Landscapers designed and constructed elaborate Japanese gardens, for example,

Families furnished their compact living spaces with scraps and ingenuity (above, an apartment in Puyallup Assembly Center, Washington state). Suitcases could double as bedside tables. Discarded bits of lumber became shelves and chairs. Camp schools required adaptation, too (below, Santa Anita Assembly Center, Calif.) Background image: A letter sent to Mary in Iowa by her mother.

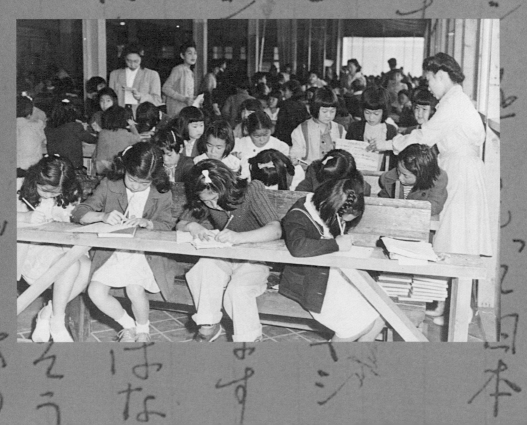

borrowing rocks from the desert landscape and using local irrigation to create interconnected pools of moving water. Other residents took jobs in camp kitchens, hospitals, schools, and workshops. They represented their neighborhood blocks as camp leaders. They staffed the camps' churches and temples. They published camp newspapers and opened libraries. They volunteered to teach craft, language, and activity classes to adult inmates. They organized dances and sporting events. And, when the confinement of the prison camps overwhelmed their attempts to feel connected to their old lives, they took comfort by reminding themselves: *Shigata ganai*. It can't be helped.

Camp schools opened in the fall of 1942, and Mary enrolled as a senior at Tule Lake's Tri-State High School. Students and teachers made do in classrooms that often lacked blackboards, textbooks, writing materials, even desks. Mary recalls learning how to type on imaginary typewriters Students pretended to mix chemicals that they did not have and envision results they could not see. A familiar school-morning ritual took on bizarre ironies as the students recited the Pledge of Allegiance to a nation, "....indivisible, with liberty and justice for all."

Then came the loyalty tests. In early 1943 the government developed plans for releasing many of its prisoners. Some had already been permitted to leave camps temporarily to help with essential farm work or to attend college. Now officials were ready to let others leave permanently; they just needed to decide who could be trusted. Authorities prepared an "Application for Leave Clearance" form and asked every person over the age of 17 to complete it. The document seemed routine until respondents reached questions 27 and 28. These items, with the clumsiest of wording, asked applicants if they would be loyal to the United States. Young male Nisei adults were singled out, even as they sat confined behind barbed wire, and asked if they would willingly serve in the U.S. military.

"Are these trick questions?" Mary and others wondered. The form "was confusing and terrifying, creating paranoia among the internees," she recalls. Would camp residents have to leave camp if they answered "Yes Yes" to questions 27 and 28? Where could they go, since they could not yet return to the restricted zones along the West Coast? Should a young man have to risk his life in order to prove his loyalty? What debt of loyalty did someone owe to a country that had taken away his freedom? What would happen to the people who dared to answer "No No"? Would they be jailed? Deported to Japan? Tensions ran high, especially at Tule Lake, where groups of "No No boys" pressured undecided youths to join them. People preparing to answer "Yes Yes" kept quiet to avoid harassment.

Mary's family debated how best to respond. "It is important for me to maintain faith that this will all work out eventually for the best," decided Mr. Matsuda. "I choose to vote 'Yes Yes.'" Mary's mother

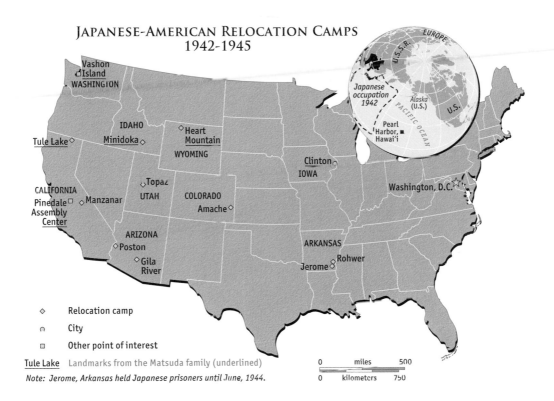

JAPANESE-AMERICAN RELOCATION CAMPS
1942-1945

Vashon Island
WASHINGTON

IDAHO

Tule Lake ◇
Minidoka ◇

◇ Heart Mountain

WYOMING

Clinton ◌
IOWA

Washington, D.C. ☆

◇ Topaz
CALIFORNIA
UTAH
Pinedale ☐ ◇ Manzanar
Assembly
Center

COLORADO
Amache ◇

ARIZONA
◇ Poston

ARKANSAS
◇ Rohwer
Jerome ◇

◇ Gila River

Japanese
occupation
1942
Alaska (U.S.)
PACIFIC OCEAN
Pearl Harbor, ■
Hawai'i
U.S.
EUROPE
U.S.S.R.

◇   Relocation camp

◌   City

☐   Other point of interest

Tule Lake   Landmarks from the Matsuda family (underlined)

Note: Jerome, Arkansas held Japanese prisoners until June, 1944.

| 0 | miles | 500 |
| 0 | kilometers | 750 |

Members of the Matsuda family lived at three of the government's ten Japanese-American relocation camps during World War II. "I didn't know there could be so many bleak and barren places in this country," Mary observed then.

agreed. Yoneichi observed: "My 'Yes Yes' decision will mean I must go into the army and fight in the war.…..That is the one thing I can do to prove our family's loyalty to the United States." Mary's anger and sense of betrayal left her tempted to vote "No No." "Although I knew 'Yes Yes' was the right choice, it broke my heart," she writes in *Looking Like the Enemy*. "It felt like giving in to the bully in the schoolyard."

Most respondents answered "Yes Yes" to the controversial questions, but 10,000 people out of nearly 75,000 did not. Some of these people

Mary (at left, in uniform with her brother) helped her mother make Yoneichi a senninbari to protect him in battle. The traditional ceremonial cloth belt was topped with 1,000 stitches sewn using a continuous thread. Mary and her mother sewed the first two stitches themselves. Then they recruited 998 women to help them complete the belt.

were eventually deported or sought to leave the U.S. Most remained, but an invisible, long-lasting dividing line of tension developed between them and other members of the Japanese-American community. "It took me more than 50 years to understand and appreciate the sacrifices of those who chose 'No No,'" Mary admits in her memoir. "The 'No No' people fought for our rights in a very different way.... Dissent is an essential expression of democracy."

Yoneichi learned in the spring of 1944 that he would be shipping out for military training at the end of June. He became part of the U.S. Army's 442nd Regimental Combat Team, a segregated force fighting in

Europe made up entirely of Japanese Americans. His regiment became one of the most highly decorated forces during the war, with soldiers earning more than 18,000 medals. In all, some 23,000 Japanese American citizens fought on the side of the United States during World War II.

Mary, by then a high school graduate, chose a form of wartime service, too. She applied to become a member of the U.S. Cadet Nurse Corps through training at a teaching hospital in Clinton, Iowa. She enrolled in the three-year program that fall and was still in training during August 1945 when the war came to a close. The fighting ended, as it had begun, with a shocking use of aerial bombing—in this case the destruction by atomic weapons of two of Japan's major cities.

Even before that point the U.S. government had begun emptying its relocation camps. Officials gave departing internees $25 each and the funds to cover transportion from the camp. With military restrictions at last lifted on the West Coast, most people headed back toward familiar ground. The Matsudas were among the lucky ones; they had managed to hold onto their farm. Many families had no place left to call home. The government established a small compensation fund, but it did not begin to cover the losses of the entire Japanese-American community. *Shigata ganai.* It can't be helped, or at least it did not seem so at the time. Yoneichi survived the war. He came home in 1946 with a Bronze Star. By the time Mary returned to Vashon Island in 1947, she had not seen her family for more than two years or her home for more than five.

More than three decades passed before President Gerald R. Ford initiated the process of apologizing for the Japanese American incarceration. In 1976 he symbolically revoked Executive Order 9066 on the 34th anniversary of its signing. "We know now what we should have known then," asserted Ford. "Not only was that evacuation wrong, but Japanese Americans were and are loyal Americans." Ford called for "an honest reckoning" of "our national mistakes."

It would take 13 years, three more Presidents, a comprehensive study, and two acts of Congress before Ford's reckoning would be complete. As it unfolded, stories poured out from survivors of the prison camps who had kept silent for decades about their hardships and humiliations. Finally, in 1990, the government began issuing checks of $20,000 to each camp survivor along with a letter of apology signed by President George Bush.

The apology came too late for many of the former prisoners. Mary's parents and brother were dead when she received her letter. Her mother had died at age 73 two dozen years before. Her father survived another five years, reaching the age of 93. Both had been able to become U.S. citizens. Yoneichi, a school teacher, husband, and father, kept the Matsuda farm running until his death in 1985 at age 62. The farm remains in the family today. Mary became the wife of

Wartime service by Japanese Americans (above, members of the 442nd regiment) helped defuse some of the country's longtime anti-Japanese racism. "You fought not only the enemy," said President Harry S. Truman when Yoneichi's unit returned to America in July 1946. "You fought prejudice and you have won."

a minister and the mother of three children. She worked as a nurse for more than 25 years, establishing a phone-in nurses' hotline that inspired the creation of similar programs nationwide. In 2002, she was one of a handful of delegates chosen to discuss healthcare matters during a conference with President George W. Bush, the son of the President who had apologized for her imprisonment.

A growing number of museums and memorials help document

The National Japanese American Memorial to Patriotism opened in Washington, D.C., in 2000. It honors Japanese Americans imprisoned in the U.S. during World War II as well as those who served in the nation's military. Among those commemorated by the memorial was Daniel Inouye (left), a veteran of the Second World War who went on to become a U.S. Senator.

the painful history of Japanese-American incarceration, from a monument in Washington, D.C., to a national historic site in southeastern California at the Manzanar camp. An exhibit there posts a mirror at child height and asks: "Who were these people like?" The answer, of course, is that the imprisoned people, until they were scooped up and incarcerated, were as ordinary and carefree as Mary Matsuda on the morning of Pearl Harbor Day, and as ordinary and carefree as today's visitors to the museum.

Historian Roger Daniels notes how the injustices faced by these victims of prejudice "is an ironic and disgraceful aspect of a war whose stated objective was freedom." He asks: "Could it happen again?" Daniels cites a series of examples where the U.S. government has reacted harshly during perceived security threats. His list includes the passage of the Emergency Detention Act in 1950 that authorized the creation of permanent camps for suspected troublemakers, the detention of illegal Haitian immigrants during the 1980s (while illegal Cuban immigrants were openly welcomed), and the ethnically-based questioning during the Persian Gulf War of Arab Americans, including U.S. citizens. (Similar accusations were leveled at people of Middle Eastern origin during the Iraq War.) Americans tend "to react against 'foreigners' in the United States in times of crisis," he concludes, "especially when those foreigners have dark skin."

The day before Mary Matsuda Gruenewald spoke at the White House with George W. Bush, she visited the National Japanese American Memorial to Patriotism near the U.S. Capitol. That evening she realized the symbolism of the day's date, May 16, 2002. Exactly 60 years before, she and Yoneichi and her parents had become Family Number 19788.

"WHEN WE WANT YOU, WE'LL CALL YOU; WHEN WE DON'T—GIT."

U.S. RANCHER,

ADDRESSING A MEXICAN WORKER CIRCA 1927

"I have worked all my life, and all I have now is my broken body," a Mexican told Dorothea Lange as she photographed migrant laborers in California during 1935 (above, Lange's image of a Mexican field worker, the father of six children). Background image: Trains deliver Mexican workers to California to help with crop harvesting during World War II.

EXPLOITED
"When We Want You, We'll Call You"

MORE THAN 150 YEARS AGO THE UNITED STATES FOUGHT with Mexico over the control of vast territories along a shared border. The U.S. came out ahead and claimed the land that would eventually form some or all of eight new states. Most of the region's 80,000 or so Mexican residents chose to stay put. They became some of the nation's first Mexican Americans. Patterns of migration across the nearly 2,000-mile-long border between the two countries have defined this area ever since. But shifting boundary lines, changing rules, and varying security measures have made less difference over the years than a basic law of human nature: if people want to cross a border badly enough, they probably will.

Push and pull—those forces that brought immigrants from China to California and refugees from Nazi Germany to the shores of the United States—prompted the first major wave of Mexican border crossings in the early 20th century, too. The Mexican Revolution and unemployment there helped push emigrants out of their country even as job opportunities pulled them toward the United States. Increased federal restriction on the entry of cheap labor from places like China and Japan prompted employers to seek help from Mexico instead. They hired Mexicans to work in mines, at oilfields, on ranches, with railroads, and, most of all, in the spreading fields and orchards of the American Southwest. As hard as the work was, it was better than no work at all. As low as the pay was, it was higher than typical Mexican wages.

At the turn of the 20th century, the border between the United States and Mexico stood largely unguarded. People passed easily and frequently between the two nations in a region that seemed more united by its shared culture and history than divided by a border drawn on a map. Mexicans routinely commuted to the United States and stayed for a season of work, then returned home after the harvest with the money that would help support their families until the next cycle of work began. Some even chose to settle permanently in the United States; they helped establish barrios, or Latino neighborhoods, in cities like Los Angeles.

The advent of World War I pulled a second wave of Mexicans into

Border security was a relaxed affair some 100 years ago, perhaps with just a few guards stationed at informal checkpoints (above, Brownsville, Texas).

the American workforce. Demand for commodities like cotton (for uniforms) and food (for a growing army) led to the planting of even more acres of crops. Mexicans and Mexican Americans—people of Mexican heritage who had immigrated to the United States or been born there—filled vacant jobs in Southwestern fields as well as in the factories of distant urban areas. They established Latino communities

"If I could earn $4 a week, we could get along," this Mexican worker told photographer Dorothea Lange when she visited his camp for migrant laborers in 1935.

in such places as Chicago, Detroit, and St. Louis while providing essential wartime labor to the United States and its allies. After the war Mexicans were sloughed to the bottom of the labor market in the same way that the Chinese were marginalized when their help was no longer needed to build the Western railroads. The U.S. government deported many of the unemployed Mexicans, often with the help of their former employers. The Ford Motor Company, for example, sent 3,000 nationals back to Mexico.

This cycle of migration, hiring, firing, and exploitation has repeated itself with regularity ever since. Mexicans who were pulled back to the United States by the economic boom of the so-called Roaring '20s, for instance, found themselves less welcome after the arrival of the Great Depression in the 1930s. Signs might proclaim: "No niggers, Mexicans, or dogs allowed," and some states passed laws limiting certain jobs to U.S. citizens. Employers often failed to distinguish between Mexican American citizens and non-citizens. Deportations began again. The forced departure of one family member, especially a breadwinner, often triggered the exodus of other relatives, even children with U.S. citizenship.

"They gave you a choice," one immigrant living in Indiana noted wryly, "starve or go back to Mexico." Los Angeles filled 16 trains bound for Mexico in the early 1930s, for example. Instead of using passenger cars, the city packed more than 13,000 Mexicans and Mexican Americans into freight boxcars.

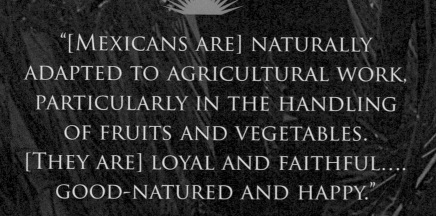

"[MEXICANS ARE] NATURALLY ADAPTED TO AGRICULTURAL WORK, PARTICULARLY IN THE HANDLING OF FRUITS AND VEGETABLES. [THEY ARE] LOYAL AND FAITHFUL.... GOOD-NATURED AND HAPPY."

CHARLES TEAGUE, PRESIDENT
CALIFORNIA FRUIT GROWERS EXCHANGE, 1944

Mexicans filled back-breaking farm jobs (at work in a tomato field) in order to stay employed during the Depression.

The revolving door reversed direction during the Second World War when U.S. farmers and industrial leaders called for a return of the Mexican workforce. A wiser and warier Mexican government insisted on establishing worker safeguards before permitting its citizens to cross back into the United States. In 1942 the U.S. pledged that participants in its new bracero program (named using a Spanish term for hired hands) would receive guaranteed wages and other job security in exchange for filling wartime labor shortages in America's fields and factories.

This third wave of Mexican workers arrived in the U.S. via passenger trains. At first none traveled to Texas because Mexico refused to subject braceros to the state's exceptionally abusive work environment. Many braceros filled jobs on the West Coast where Japanese Americans had previously worked; those laborers now resided behind barbed wire in U.S. government internment camps. An uncounted number of Mexicans chose to enter the U.S. outside of the bracero program, too. They took whatever jobs they could find wherever they could find them—including Texas.

After World War II, the U.S. government extended the bracero program through peacetime and another war (in Korea) in order to fill jobs in the expanding U.S. labor market. Not until 1964 did the bracero program come to an end in response to increased mechanization, growing protests against the harsh working conditions of braceros, and diminished influence in Washington by agricultural interests. By then Mexicans had filled as many as five million bracero jobs.

Even before the program ended, though, the U.S. government took steps to remove illegal Mexican immigrants from the country's labor markets. A 1954 effort reflected both the increased power of labor unions (who believed cheap labor from Mexico undercut their own demands for higher wages) as well as heightened concern over national security (during the Cold War with the Soviet Union). Thus was born "Operation Wetback," a program named using the derogatory term for Mexican immigrants who had entered the U.S. illegally, perhaps by swimming the border's Rio Grande River and literally getting wet. The program prompted a million people or more to leave the U.S. because of intimidation and fear of prosecution. Once again families and young U.S. citizens were uprooted.

The death of the bracero program in 1964 gave life to the next wave of Mexican travelers: an expanding flow of illegal immigrants. By this time hundreds of thousands of Mexican families over several generations had become part of a cross-border economy. Bracero program or not, many Mexicans depended on finding work in the United States every year. U.S. growers, in particular, were equally dependent on hiring back the people they viewed as reliable, hard-working, and affordable. As back-breaking as the work was, as low as the wages were, and as challenging as the trip might become, Mexicans kept commuting north to work.

United States officials tolerated, even welcomed, a certain amount of illegal traffic. Many Mexican workers who "slipped in" at the beginning of the harvest season willingly gave themselves up for deportation when it ended, so they could fly home at government expense. Their capture allowed the border patrol to boast of impressive enforcement efforts.

Groups of wartime braceros traveled via trains in a seasonal migration that took place between their homes in Mexico and the jobs they found in the United States.

Mexicans helped with agricultural work (left, harvesting beets) during World War II. They took the place of Americans who had stepped into jobs created by the war effort at home and abroad.

The revolving cycle of immigration between Mexico and the United States continues today even as the population of Mexican Americans and other Latinos swells to influential proportions. Battle lines can be quickly drawn between members of the Latino community, nativists who fear the influence of this newest immigrant population, employers who favor continued access to inexpensive hired help, labor unions who resent the way immigrant labor keeps their own wages lower, civil rights forces who argue for greater protection from worker exploitation, and politicians who seem to side with whichever group becomes loudest and most influential.

Arguments develop over questions that have no simple answers. Do Mexicans and other illegal immigrants fill jobs that could be held by U.S. citizens? Or do they do work that would go otherwise undone or be shipped overseas? Can a nation ever really secure a border that is nearly 2,000 miles long? Does increased border security have the unintended consequence of encouraging Mexicans who reach the U.S. to stop commuting and thus remain permanently (and illegally) in America? Do migrant workers contribute more to the society than they take away? Should amnesty be given to the millions of illegal immigrants in the United States? Or would amnesty just encourage more immigrants to enter the country illegally in hopes of future forgiveness? Is the nation of immigrants full?

Such debates can distract people from a more basic dimension of the situation: the U.S. and Mexican economies have been linked in a sometimes exploitative, sometimes beneficial cycle for a century. The countries may be divided by an international border, but one community of work and heritage overlies the region. The issue boils down to the forces of push and pull. Until economic conditions change so that Mexicans have incentives to remain in their home country, they will continue to cross the border to work in the United States. How the U.S. copes with this reality will help determine the next round of immigration legislation—and the nature of the next wave of arriving immigrants.

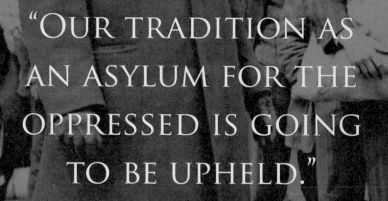

> "OUR TRADITION AS AN ASYLUM FOR THE OPPRESSED IS GOING TO BE UPHELD."

PRESIDENT LYNDON B. JOHNSON,
UPON SIGNING THE IMMIGRATION ACT OF 1965

The United States has been alternately welcoming and hostile to those who have tried to cross through "the golden door" into America. Background image: Immigrants prepare to enter the United States via Ellis Island, 1911.

AFTERWORD

THAT "MIGHTY WOMAN WITH A TORCH" FROM EMMA Lazarus's poem continues to symbolize the promise of the American Dream even as waves of immigrants have failed to find shelter or acceptance within the United States. Naomi Shihab Nye opened this book with a poem that voices a sentiment many might wish the Statue of Liberty to share today: "Any chance I could be, again, the one I used to be?" Can the nation "bring back a shine" to liberty's torchlight for what Lazarus called "the golden door"?

The cycle of U.S. immigration history is marked with many changes in the standing of that door. Forces have narrowed its width, as they did in 1924 with the development of the quota system, and they have broadened it dramatically with benchmark legislation like the Immigration Act of 1965. Evolving laws and statistics help measure the shifting hinge of immigration history, but the numbers

Even the popular phrase "immigration reform" has taken on two contradictory meanings. Careful students of the subject must ask: Is the reform intended to protect immigrants, or is it designed to keep them out? The 1901 plea of Chinese diplomat Wu Ting-fang echoes through the debate: "Why can't you be fair?"

come alive in the stories of people like Emma Goldman, Herb Karliner, and Mary Matsuda Gruenewald whose lives were so affected by the nation's changing immigration policies. Inevitably, given enough time, even those immigrant groups who once were greeted with fear and scorn—from Russians to German Jews to Japanese—have become accepted as part of the American family. Debates today focus on newcomers not yet woven into the national fabric.

What refuge does the United States owe to Iraqi citizens who supported the U.S. invasion of their country but then had to flee their homes because of the dangers that the American intervention helped to create? Iraqis still live in exile awaiting their turn to cross through the golden door of American immigration.

What protections might Americans be asked to forfeit when their heritage makes them suspect during a time of war? Immigrants from the Middle East languished in jails for years following the September 11 terrorist attacks with only limited access to legal advice and endless delays of their rights to hear charges and stand trial.

What respect is due to illegal immigrants who toil at the nation's meanest jobs in exchange for its poorest wages? Even today Latinos are snatched from their homes and places of work, arrested, and often deported regardless of their contributions to the American workplace and their ties to their American-born children.

Denied, detained, deported. These stories from the 21st century illustrate how the cycle of exclusion and exploitation endures. Only when citizens uphold the promise of America's founders does the cycle turn away from the dark side. Each generation decides what face it wants the nation to wear. Its leaders must weigh matters with their heads and their hearts as they search for the best answers to the immigration puzzles of their day.

Every so often they honor the promise George Washington made at the conclusion of the Revolutionary War: "The bosom of America is open to receive not only the opulent and respectable stranger, but the oppressed and persecuted of all nations and religions." When Americans uphold this pledge, the lady's lamp shines brightly at the nation's golden door.

TIME LINE

The following time line presents major events in the history of U.S. immigration policy. Important personal elements of the immigration stories shared in this book are interspersed with the larger chronology.

1788 The U.S. Constitution calls for Congress to "establish a uniform rule of naturalization." Immigrants are eligible to serve in all federal offices except as President and Vice President.

• Congress passes a statute limiting the right for immigrants to earn citizenship through naturalization to "free white persons," thus excluding imported slaves and indentured servants from citizenship.

1798 Congress passes the Alien and Sedition Acts during the administration of John Adams. These measures allow aliens to be jailed, and even deported, for criticizing the government, but they are condemned and fall out of favor.

1819 Congress (above, the U.S. Capitol Building, circa 1890s) requires all ships entering U.S. ports to provide a list of the ship's passengers prior to passing through customs.

1870 In July Congress, through the Naturalization Act of 1870, enacts legislation that prevents Chinese immigrants from qualifying for citizenship; at the same time immigrants from Africa gain that right.

• Alexander Berkman is born on November 21 in Vilnius, Lithuania, part of the Russian Empire.

1875 The Page Act prohibits the immigration of Asian women for forced work as prostitutes.

1880 President Rutherford B. Hayes, responding to pressure from Congress, re-negotiates the Burlingame Treaty of 1868 so that the U.S. can restrict the entry of Chinese immigrants into America.

1882 The so-called Chinese Exclusion Act (officially known as the Immigration Act of 1882), marks the beginning of U.S. immigration restrictions by prohibiting further immigration from China for ten years. The act allows immigrants already in the

U.S. to travel freely between their native and adopted homelands.

1885 Emma Goldman arrives as a 16-year-old immigrant in the United States on December 29.

1886 Anarchists are held responsible for the deaths of seven Chicago police officers during a labor demonstration in the city's Haymarket Square on May 4. Four of them are executed on November 11 of the following year.

1887 Emma Goldman gains U.S. citizenship through her marriage to Jacob Kershner.

1888 Alexander Berkman emigrates to the United States in February at the age of 17.

1889 Emma Goldman and Alexander Berkman (below in 1892) meet on August 15 in a New York restaurant.

1900 Following the Spanish-American War of 1898, the Foraker Act offers national status (but not citizenship) to residents of Puerto Rico.

1903 The assassination of President William McKinley in 1901 by an American citizen (and self-proclaimed anarchist) with a foreign-sounding name leads to legislation that

can deny entry to immigrants who are judged as having radical beliefs.

1906 Congress enacts legislation that requires all future candidates for U.S. citizenship to be able to "speak the English language."

• Alexander Berkman is released from prison on May 18 after serving 14 years of his sentence.

• The decision on Oct. 6 by the San Francisco School Board to require Japanese-American students to attend segregated schools for Chinese immigrants provokes a diplomatic crisis between Japan and the U.S. President Theodore Roosevelt, conscious of Japan's military strength, signs a series of documents with Japan in 1907 and 1908 known as the

DENIED, DETAINED, DEPORTED

1848 The United States assumes control over vast territories seized from Mexico during the Mexican War. The final boundary between the two nations is settled in 1853 with the Gadsden Purchase.

1849 The U.S. Supreme Court rules in the *Passenger Cases* that the regulation of immigration is a federal responsibility, not a state one.

1850s Chinese begin to immigrate to the U.S., particularly to California (above, children in San Francisco, 1921).

1868 The ratification of the 14th Amendment to the U.S. Constitution defines citizenship as a right earned by "all persons born or naturalized in the United States." Neither race nor national origin are cited as reasons for exclusion from citizenship.

• China and the U.S. sign the Burlingame Treaty, agreeing to the "inalienable right of man to change his home and allegiance."

1869 Thousands of Chinese workers lose their jobs when the Union Pacific and the Central Pacific Railroads unite the continent at Promontory Point, Utah, on May 10.

• Emma Goldman is born on June 27 in Kovno, Lithuania, part of the Russian Empire (right, Goldman in 1918).

1891 Henry Cabot Lodge, a Republican congressman from Massachusetts, proposes for the first time that immigrants be subject to a literacy test as a condition for admission to the United States. His legislation fails.

• Congress passes immigration legislation that identifies types of immigrants who may be denied entry, such as "idiots, insane persons, paupers...persons suffering from a loathsome or a dangerous contagious disease," felons, polygamists, and so on. The ruling became known as the LPC clause, short for a phrase that included the words "likely to become a public charge" among the reasons to keep someone out.

• With the Immigration Act of 1891 Congress establishes the Bureau of Immigration within the Treasury Department and places all authority over this work in federal hands. By 1913 this work is housed at the Department of Labor along with a separate Bureau of Naturalization.

1892 Ellis Island opens on January 1 as the immigration entry point to New York City.

• In May Congress passes the Geary Act, extending for another ten years the provisions of the 1882 Chinese Exclusion Act.

• On September 19 Alexander Berkman is sentenced to serve 22 years in prison for attempting to assassinate Henry Clay Frick on July 23 following labor disputes over a steel mill strike in Homestead, Penn.

1893 Emma Goldman spends a year in jail for urging unemployed workers to riot in protest of their situation.

1894 Young graduates of Harvard University found the Immigration Restriction League and use their influence to inflame fears about immigrants, thus fueling public support for more restrictive legislation.

1898 Heisuke Matsuda, Mary Matsuda's father, immigrates to the United States from Japan.

Gentleman's Agreement. The plan limits immigration from Japan while protecting Japanese Americans.

1907 The Immigration Act of 1907 establishes a commission headed by Senator William P. Dillingham, a Republican from Vermont. The Dillingham Commission helps to develop a national quota system that limits the number of immigrants who enter the U.S. from Eastern and Southern Europe. (Right, immigrant children reach Ellis Island, 1908.)

• The Expatriation Act of 1907 strips women of their American citizenship if they marry non-citizens. Male citizens who marry non-citizen women are not penalized.

1910 Angel Island opens as the immigration entry point for San Francisco, Calif.

1917 On April 6 the United States declares war on Germany and enters World War I. Fighting continues until November 1918.

• As part of the Immigration Act of 1917, Congress overrides a presidential veto by Woodrow Wilson and passes a reading test requirement for all immigrants over 16 years of age. Married and dependent women are exempted. Literacy may be demonstrated in English or one's native language. Several previous attempts to establish a literacy test for immigrants had failed.

- Authorities arrest Emma Goldman and Alexander Berkman on June 15, charging them with conspiracy to urge violation of mandatory registration for military service. They are found guilty on July 9 and sentenced to serve two years in federal prison, pending appeals. They begin serving their sentences the following year.

  1919 On November 7 authorities round up more than 1,000 suspected radicals

during the so-called Palmer raids, simultaneous arrests in over a dozen U.S. cities.

- Emma Goldman and Alexander Berkman, just recently released from prison, are ordered on November 29 to surrender themselves for deportation at Ellis Island on December 5.

- On December 21 the military transport ship *Buford* (above) departs New York bound for Russia carrying Emma Goldman, Alexander Berkman, and 247 other alien deportees.

  1921 The Immigration Act of 1921 puts into place a temporary quota system for determining the number of immigrants who may be

admitted from various countries. The initial one-year limits are extended to cover 1922 and 1923, as well.

- Emma Goldman and Alexander Berkman grow dissatisfied with the leadership of Soviet Russia and emigrate from their homeland for the second time; they settle eventually in France.

- Mitsuno Horiye marries Heisuke Matsuda; she immigrates to the United States from Japan the next year.

- The collapse of the New York Stock Exchange market in October contributes to worldwide economic hardship—the Great Depression— which lasts for a decade.

  1933 The federal government merges the former Bureaus of Immigration and Naturalization into a new Immigration and

Naturalization Service (INS) under the jurisdiction of the Department of Labor. (In 1940 the Justice Department takes over management of the INS.)

- Adolf Hitler (left, in 1935) is named chancellor of Germany on January 30. By August 1934 he has become the nation's dictator.

  1934 Emma Goldman tours the U.S. on a three-month-long lecture tour using a temporary visa granted by the U.S. government.

  1936 Hitler, in defiance of World War I treaties, re-fortifies Germany's borders with troops. Anti-Semitism accelerates in Germany.

- Alexander Berkman dies on June 28 at the age of 65 in Nice, France. Terminally ill with cancer, he ultimately dies from a self-inflicted gunshot wound.

  1938 German troops take possession of Austria on March 12. Hitler assumes partial control of neighboring Czechoslovakia later that year, and full control by March of 1939.

- Emma Goldman dies on May 14 at the age of 70 in Toronto, Canada. Her remains are buried in Chicago, Ill., near the executed anarchists of the Haymarket Square riot.

  1941 Herb Karliner travels behind German lines in occupied France for what becomes his final visit with his parents and sisters.

- The Japanese, as allies of Germany, bomb Pearl Harbor, Hawaii, on December 7, setting the stage for the entry of America into World War II—and for the detention of Japanese Americans in the U.S. (left, banner headline).

  1942 President Franklin D. Roosevelt signs Executive Order 9066 on February 19 ordering the evacuation and detention of all Japanese Americans from vast regions of the West Coast. (Right, evacuees from Bainbridge Island, Washington state, March 30, 1942.)

- The Matsuda family is one of 37 families evicted from their homes on Vashon Island, Wash., on May 16 and

1922 Congress passes the Cable Act, eliminating the 1907 requirement that female U.S. citizens who marry non-citizens will lose their own citizenship. U.S. women who marry Asians continue to forfeit their citizenship, however. The act ends the practice of automatically granting citizenship to women who are married to U.S. citizens, too.

1924 The Immigration Act of 1924 makes permanent the principle of fixed immigration quotas for various countries, with limits determined through a special study in time to take effect in 1929. By basing the quotas on immigration patterns of 1890, the act attempts to reverse the more recent increases in immigration from Eastern and Southern Europe. The act adds Japanese to the list of Asians who are ineligible for citizenship.

1925 Mary Matsuda is born on January 23, 1925, in Seattle, Wash., two years after her brother Yoneichi. The family moves to Vashon Island, Wash., in 1927.

1926 Herbert Karliner (left, early 1930s) is born on September 3 in Peiskretscham, Germany.

1929 On July 1, per the Immigration Act of 1924, the U.S. government implements the use of quotas based on national origin to determine which immigrants may enter the country.

- Nazi guards destroy Jewish-owned property at locations throughout Germany on *Kristallnacht,* the "Night of Broken Glass," November 9. Guards destroy the Karliner family business and arrest Herbert Karliner's father.

1939 The Karliner family makes plans to flee Germany and immigrate to the United States by way of Cuba.

- On May 5 the President of Cuba eliminates the option to enter the country on tourist landing permits, as offered earlier that year in Decree 55.

- The *St. Louis* departs Hamburg, Germany, on May 13 with 937 passengers bound for Havana, Cuba. The ship reaches Havana's harbor on May 27.

- The *St. Louis* departs Havana on June 2 with all but 29 of its passengers still aboard. On June 3 the ship sights Miami, Florida, but does not dock.

- The *St. Louis* begins to re-cross the Atlantic on June 7. On June 13, word reaches the passengers of safe harbors in Europe. The ship docks at Antwerp, Belgium, on June 17 where passengers disembark to take refuge in that country, France, the United Kingdom, and the Netherlands. The Karliner family travels to France.

- Hitler invades Poland on September 1, setting off the beginning of World War II.

1940 The Alien Registration Act of 1940 requires all aliens to be fingerprinted and registered with the U.S. government; aliens are required to keep the government informed of their home address. (Protest by

We Did Not FINGERPRINT
THE PILGRIMS
WHEN THEY ARRIVED
IN OUR OWN -
NATIVE AMERICA

members of the Iroquois nation, above.)

- On May 10 German forces invade Western Europe. The Netherlands and Belgium surrender by month's end, and much of France falls under Nazi rule on June 22.

transported to the first of a series of detention camps. They remain at Pinedale Assembly Center in California from May 19 to June 30 before being transferred to Tule Lake in California.

- Congress institutes the bracero program to encourage citizens of Mexico and neighboring countries to temporarily enter the United States to fill job openings created during World War II. The program remains in effect, with modifications, through 1964.

- On August 26, authorities begin rounding up Jews in the unoccupied regions of southern France. Herb Karliner escapes detention by being under the age of 16—by seven days. By November, German forces have occupied the remainder of France.

- On November 6 Herb Karliner's mother and sisters are detained and transported to concentration camps, eventually reaching Auschwitz where they perish. His father, who is ill in Paris, meets the same fate in Auschwitz in late 1943.

1943 Government officials begin distributing questionnaires to interned Japanese Americans to determine their loyalty to the United States.

- Allied forces (the U.S., the United Kingdom, France, and Russia) invade Sicily on July 10, beginning their campaign to liberate Europe from control by the Axis powers of Germany and Italy.

• Herb Karliner takes on an assumed identity to escape detection by Nazi troops in France.

• Based on their responses to the government's loyalty questionnaire, the Matsuda family is transferred in September from Tule Lake (which becomes a center for "No No" inmates) to Heart Mountain, in Wyoming. (Left, Mary Matsuda at age 22 following World War II.)

• At the request of President Franklin D. Roosevelt, Congress repeals in December old statutes that restricted Chinese immigration and naturalization.

1944 Yoneichi Matsuda begins military service for World War II combat; Mary Matsuda enrolls for training to join the U.S. Cadet Nurse Corps. Their parents relocate to Minidoka Relocation Camp in Idaho.

1945 Adolf Hitler commits suicide on April 30. On May 7 Germany surrenders.

• Even as World War II draws to a close, the U.S. extends the wartime bracero program (below, braceros, 1943). The program lasts through 1964.

• In August the United States drops atomic bombs on the Japanese cities of Hiroshima and Nagasaki (above). Japan's subsequent surrender ends World War II on August 15.

• President Harry S. Truman, who unsuccessfully vetoed the INA as too restrictive, establishes a commission to study the nation's immigration policies. Its report, *Whom We Shall Welcome*, prompts changes to U.S. policy during the next decade.

1953 Congress passes the Refugee Relief Act, enabling almost 200,000 immigrants to enter the U.S. without regard to national quotas.

1954 U.S. officials seek to identify and deport illegal Mexican immigrants through a program called "Operation Wetback."

• Mitsuno Matsuda and Heisuke Matsuda pass the exam that makes them U.S. citizens.

1956 The Immigration and Naturalization Service develops a "Chinese Confession Program" to weed out individuals with phony citizenship papers by granting amnesty to informants whose own records are often questionable, too.

1957 Congress passes the Refugee-Escapee Act, allowing more people to be counted as refugees when immigrating to the U.S.

1960 Congress passes the Fair Share Refugee Act, clarifying reasons for excluding individuals from admission to the U.S.

1962 Congress passes the Migration and Refugee Assistance Act of 1962 to facilitate easier entry by Cubans into the U.S.

1965 The Immigration Act of 1965 revolutionizes U.S. immigration policy by ending the old quota system developed during the 1920s. The act establishes quotas for the globe's Eastern and Western Hemispheres, expands the opportunity for family members to follow initial immigrants to the country, and increases the ease with which refugees can enter the country.

1992 Congress passes the Chinese Student Protection Act and the Soviet Scientists Immigration Act to ensure the safe immigration of individuals at risk of persecution by authoritarian governments.

1994 California voters approve Proposition 187, a measure restricting the access of illegal immigrants to social services—including education and health care. Federal courts rule the measure unconstitutional, but debate over the provision serves to increase anti-immigrant rhetoric in the U.S.

1996 Congress passes a series of laws that increase control of the border with Mexico, reduce access by aliens to social services (such as food stamps), and tighten immigration for potential terrorists. Some provisions are later repealed as too harsh, in part because they affect citizen children born to immigrants who may be in the country illegally or without citizenship rights.

1998 The Non-Citizen Benefit Clarification Act establishes that immigrants without citizenship do qualify for some social services, such as economic assistance.

2001 Terrorists with extreme Islamic views attack the U.S. on September 11, prompting increased security concerns and heightened suspicion of immigrants.

2003 Duties of the INS and related offices are reorganized during the creation of the Department of Homeland Security into three branches of

• The War Brides Act of 1945 and a similar act passed the following year make it possible for immigrant spouses and fiancées of members of the U.S. armed services to enter the United States regardless of immigration quotas.

1947 Mary Matsuda graduates from nursing school and returns to Vashon Island, Wash., in July; her parents had moved back to their farm in September 1945 and her brother in June 1946.

• Herbert Karliner and his brother Walter immigrate to the United States.

1948 The Displaced Persons Act establishes the nation's first program specifically designed to serve refugees. Thousands of postwar immigrants are admitted without regard to quotas. A similar act passes in 1950.

1950 Congress overrides the presidential veto of Harry S. Truman (above) by passing the Internal Security Act of 1950 to guard against perceived threats to national security by communists and fascists.

1952 The McCarran-Walter Act, also known as the Immigration and Nationality Act (INA), removes barriers to immigration and naturalization based on race and ethnic background, thus ending the exclusion of Asian immigrants from these rights. Other provisions of the bill extend the practice of immigration quotas, limit the admission of political radicals, and make deportations easier.

1976 President Gerald R. Ford acknowledges the mistake of the Japanese American internment during World War II and initiates efforts that lead to a formal apology and the issuing of $20,000 reparation checks to camp survivors beginning in 1990.

1980 The Refugee Act of 1980 offers asylum protection for individuals already in the United States who can document that their well being would be threatened if they returned to their home countries.

• The sudden lifting of emigration restrictions by Cuban leader Fidel Castro prompts Cubans to flee their homeland in boats and makeshift rafts from the port of Mariel. (Above, passengers arrive on a shrimp boat.) This

so-called Mariel Boatlift floods the United States with tens of thousands of unexpected refugees until Castro reinstates tighter emigration procedures.

1986 The Immigration Reform and Control Act (IRCA) tightens some provisions of the more welcoming Immigration Reform Act of 1965 so that fewer immigrants arrive from the countries of Asia and Latin America. At the same time, the act grants amnesty and residency to some 2.7 million formerly illegal immigrants.

1990 The Immigration Act of 1990 expands opportunities for the admission of temporary and permanent workers, relaxes the 1952 restriction on perceived radicals, and seeks to make it harder for criminals to enter the country.

1991 Mary Matsuda Gruenewald receives a $20,000 check accompanied by a signed apology from President George Bush for her internment during World War II.

responsibility: the U.S. Citizenship and Immigration Services, the U.S. Immigration and Customs Enforcement division, and the U.S. Customs and Border Protection unit. (Right, screening international visitors, 2004.)

2007 The U.S. Congress fails to approve a comprehensive immigration reform bill despite the strong support of President George W. Bush.

RESOURCE GUIDE

BOOKS OF GENERAL INTEREST

Burton, J., M. Farrell, F. Lord, and R. Lord. *Confinement and Ethnicity: An Overview of World War II Japanese American Relocation Sites.* Online book offered through the National Park Service website:
www.nps.gov/history/history/online_books/anthropology74/cet.htm

Gruenewald, Mary Matsuda. *Looking Like the Enemy: My Story of Imprisonment in Japanese-American Internment Camps.* Troutdale, Oregon: NewSage Press, 2005.
www.lookingliketheenemy.com

Ogilvie, Sarah A. and Scott Miller. *Refuge Denied: The* St. Louis *Passengers and the Holocaust.* Madison, Wisconsin: The University of Wisconsin Press, 2006.

Oppenheim, Joanne. *Dear Miss Breed: True Stories of the Japanese American Incarceration During World War II and a Librarian Who Made a Difference.* New York, New York: Scholastic, 2006.

FILMS AND VIDEOS

"Children of the Camps" PBS documentary, 1999
www.pbs.org/childofcamp/

"Emma Goldman" American Experience documentary, 2004
www.pbs.org/wgbh/amex/goldman/index.html

"Exploring the Japanese American Internment through Film and the Internet"
http://www.asianamericanmedia.org/jainternment/

PLACES TO VISIT IN PERSON AND ONLINE

Angel Island Immigration Station
San Francisco Harbor
www.parks.ca.gov/?page_id=1309

Ellis Island Immigration Museum
Part of the Statue of Liberty National Monument, New York City Harbor
www.nps.gov/elis/

Search engine for passenger lists
www.ellisisland.org/

"The Peopling of America"
Interactive exhibit
www.ellisislandrecords.org/immexp/wseix_4_3.asp

"Emma Goldman"
Online exhibit from the Jewish Women's Archive
jwa.org/exhibits/wov/goldman/over.html

Emma Goldman Papers
University of California at Berkeley
sunsite.berkeley.edu/Goldman/

Japanese American National Museum
Clara Breed Collection
www.janm.org/django/collections/clara_breed/collection

Museum of Chinese in America
70 Mulberry Street
New York, N.Y. 10013
www.mocanyc.org/about/

U.S. Holocaust Memorial Museum
Washington, D.C.
Online exhibit about the "Voyage of the St. Louis"
www.ushmm.org/museum/exhibit/online/stlouis/

BIBLIOGRAPHY

"700 Jewish Refugees Await Fate Off Cuba." *New York Times* (New York, New York), May 28, 1939, p. L15.

"'Ark' with 300 Reds Sails Early Today for Unnamed Port." *New York Times* (New York, New York), December 21, 1919, pp. 1, 3.

Associated Press. "Coast Guard Trails Tragic Liner as It Wanders Aimless in Florida Waters." *Washington Post* (Washington, D.C.), June 5, 1939, p. 1.

———. "Cuba Orders Refugee Ship to Leave." *Washington Post* (Washington, D.C.), June 2, 1939, p. 1.

———. "Cubans May Let Refugee Ship Return." *Washington Post* (Washington, D.C.), June 4, 1939, p. 1.

———. "Refugees Quit Cuba, Buoyed By Hope U.S. Will Harbor Them." *Washington Post* (Washington, D.C.), June 3, 1939, p. 1.

"Barred in Cuba, Refugee Ship Heads Home." *Washington Post* (Washington, D.C.), June 7, 1939, p. 1.

"Burial on U.S. Soil for Emma Goldman." *New York Times* (New York, New York), May 18, 1940, p. 20.

"Convict Berkman and Miss Goldman; Both Off to Prison." *New York Times* (New York, New York), July 10, 1917, pp. 1, 8.

"Cuba Again Asked to Admit Emigres." *New York Times* (New York, New York), June 8, 1939, pp. 1, 14.

Culley, John Joel. "Enemy Alien Control in the United States During World War II: A Survey." In *Alien Justice: Wartime Internment in Australia and North America,* edited by Kay Saunders and Roger Daniels, 138-51. Queensland, Australia: University of Queensland Press, 2000.

Daniels, Roger. *Asian America: Chinese and Japanese in the United States since 1850.* Seattle, Washington: University of Washington Press, 1988.

———. *Coming to America: A History of Immigration and Ethnicity in American Life.* New York, New York: HarperCollins Publishers, 2002.

———. *Guarding the Golden Door: American Immigration Policy and Immigrants Since 1882.* New York, New York: Hill and Wang, 2004.

———. "Incarcerating Japanese-Americans: An Atrocity Revisited." In *Alien Justice: Wartime Internment in Australia and North America,* edited by Kay Saunders and Roger Daniels, 168-84. Queensland, Australia: University of Queensland Press, 2000.

———. *Not Like Us: Immigrants and Minorities in America, 1890-1924.* Chicago, Illinois: Ivan R. Dee, Inc., 1997.

Davis, Kenneth S. *FDR: Into the Storm, 1937-40, a History.* New York, New York: Random House, Inc., 1993.

"Deportation Death Is Berkman's Plea." *New York Times* (New York, New York), December 11, 1919, p. 5.

Drinnon, Richard and Anna Maria, Editors. *Nowhere at Home: Letters from Exile of Emma Goldman and Alexander Berkman.* New York, New York: Schocken Books, 1975.

"Emma Goldman, Anarchist, Dead." *New York Times* (New York, New York), May 14, 1940, p. 30.

"Endless Voyage." *Time,* June 12, 1939, pp. 22-23.

Falk, Candace. *Love, Anarchy, and Emma Goldman.* New York, New York: Holt, Rinehart and Winston, 1984.

———, Editor. *Emma Goldman, A Documentary History of the American Years: Volume 1, Made for America, 1890-1901.*

Berkeley, California: University of California Press, 2003.

"Fear Suicide Wave on Refugees' Ship." *New York Times* (New York, New York), June 1, 1939, p. L16.

Fellner, Gene, Editor. *Life of an Anarchist: The Alexander Berkman Reader.* New York, New York: Seven Stories Press, 1992, 2005.

Freidel, Frank. *Franklin D. Roosevelt: A Rendezvous with Destiny.* Boston, Massachusetts: Little, Brown and Company, 1990.

Friedlander, Saul. *Nazi Germany and the Jews: Volume I, The Years of Persecution, 1933-1939.* New York, New York: HarperCollins Publishers, 1997.

Gerhart, Ann. "Journey From Hell and Back." *Washington Post* (Washington, D.C.), April 3, 1999, p. C1.

Glassgold, Peter, Editor. *Anarchy! An Anthology of Emma Goldman's* Mother Earth. Washington, D.C.: Counterpoint, 2001.

Goldman, Emma. *Living My Life: Volume One.* New York, New York: Alfred Knopf, Inc., 1931; reproduced, New York, New York: Dover Publications, Inc., 1970.

———. *Living My Life: Volume Two.* New York, New York: Alfred Knopf, Inc., 1931; reproduced, New York, New York: Dover Publications, Inc., 1970.

Goodwin, Doris Kearns. *No Ordinary Time: Franklin and Eleanor Roosevelt, The Home Front in World War II.* New York, New York: Touchstone Books, Simon & Schuster, 1994.

Gruenewald, Mary Matsuda. *Looking Like the Enemy: My Story of Imprisonment in Japanese-American Internment Camps.* Troutdale, Oregon: NewSage Press, 2005.

Hata, Jr., Donald Teruo and Nadine Ishitani Hata. "Justice Delayed But Not Denied?" In *Alien Justice: Wartime Internment in Australia and North America,* edited by Kay Saunders and Roger Daniels, 221-33. Queensland, Australia: University of Queensland Press, 2000.

"Haven Still Sought for 907 on *St. Louis.*" *New York Times* (New York, New York), June 10, 1939, p. 9.

Hayashi, Brian Masaru. *Democratizing the Enemy: The Japanese American Internment.* Princeton, New Jersey: Princeton University Press, 2004.

"Hundreds of Reds on Soviet 'Ark' Sail Soon for Russia." *New York Times* (New York, New York), December 13, 1919, pp. 1, 2.

Inada, Lawson Fusao, Editor. *Only What We Could Carry: The Japanese American Internment Experience.* Berkeley, California: Heydey Books, 2000.

Ishizuka, Karen L. *Lost and Found: Reclaiming the Japanese American Incarceration.* Urbana, Illinois: University of Illinois Press, 2006.

Johnson, Kevin R. *The "Huddled Masses" Myth: Immigration and Civil Rights.* Philadelphia, Pennsylvania: Temple University Press, 2004.

Karliner, Herbert. Oral history interview conducted by Joe Unger, Holocaust Documentation and Education Center, Miami, Florida, 1985.

Ketchum, Richard M. *The Borrowed Years, 1938-1941: America on the Way to War.* New York, New York: Random House, Inc., 1989.

Kimball, Warren F. "The United States." In *The Origins of World War II: The Debate Continues,* edited by Robert and Joseph A. Maiolo Boyce, pp. 134-54. Basingstoke, Hampshire, England: Palgrave Macmillan, 2003.

Kraut, Alan M. *The Huddled Masses: The Immigrant in American Society, 1880-1921.* Arlington Heights, Illinois: Harlan Davidson, Inc., 1982.

Laqueur, Walter. *Generation Exodus: The Fate of Young Jewish Refugees from Nazi Germany.* Hanover, New Hampshire: Brandeis University Press, 2001.

Lawrence, David. "Friction." *The United States News* (later renamed *U.S. News and World Report*), June 5, 1939, p 14.

"Man's Inhumanity." *New York Times* (New York, New York), June 9, 1939, p. 20.

McWilliams, Carey. *Factories in the Field.* Santa Barbara, California: Peregrine Publishers, 1971 (reprint of 1935 edition).

Meier, Matt S. and Feliciano Ribera. *Mexican Americans, American Mexicans: From Conquistadors to Chicanos.* New York, New York: Hill and Wang, 1993 revised edition.

Ogilvie, Sarah A. and Scott Miller. *Refuge Denied: The* St. Louis *Passengers and the Holocaust.* Madison, Wisconsin: The University of Wisconsin Press, 2006.

Personal Justice Denied: Report of the Commission in Wartime Relocation and Internment of Civilians. Seattle, Washington: University of Washington Press, 1997.

Phillips, R. Hart. "907 Refugees Quit Cuba on Liner; Ship Reported Hovering Off Coast." *New York Times* (New York, New York), June 3, 1939, pp. 1, 4.

———. "Cuba Opens Doors to 907 on *St. Louis.*" *New York Times* (New York, New York), June 6, 1939, pp. 1, 2.

———. "Cuba Orders Liner and Refugees to Go." *New York Times* (New York, New York), June 2, 1939, pp. 1, 5.

———. "Cuba Recloses Door to Refugees." *New York Times* (New York, New York), June 7, 1939, pp. 1, 11.

"Refugee Ship Idles Off Florida Coast." *New York Times* (New York, New York), June 5, 1939, p. 1.

Robinson, Greg. *By Order of the President: FDR and the Internment of Japanese Americans.* Cambridge, Massachusetts: Harvard University Press, 2001.

Rubinstein, William D. *The Myth of Rescue.* London, England and New York, New York: Routledge, 1997.

Schmidt, Regin. *Red Scare: FBI and the Origins of Anticommunism in the United States, 1919-1943.* Copenhagen, Denmark: Museum Tusculanum Press, University of Copenhagen, 2000.

Smith, Jean Edward. *FDR.* New York, New York: Random House, 2007.

Taylor, Sandra C. "From Incarceration to Freedom: Japanese-Americans and the Departure from the Concentration Camps." In *Alien Justice: Wartime Internment in Australia and North America,* edited by Kay Saunders and Roger Daniels, 205-20. Queensland, Australia: University of Queensland Press, 2000.

Teague, Charles C. *Fifty Years a Rancher.* Los Angeles, California: Ward Ritchie Press, 1944.

Thomas, Gordon and Max Morgan Witts. *Voyage of the Damned.* Old Saybrook, Connecticut: Konecky & Konecky, 1974.

Thompson, Charles Willis. "An Interview with Emma Goldman." *New York Times* (New York, New York), May 30, 1909, Sunday Magazine, p. 7.

Tong, Benson. *The Chinese Americans.* Boulder, Colorado: University Press of Colorado, 2003.

"Tragedy Afloat." *Newsweek,* June 12, 1939, pp. 21-22.

Wexler, Alice. *Emma Goldman in America.* Boston, Massachusetts: Beacon Press, 1984.

———. *Emma Goldman In Exile: From the Russian Revolution to the Spanish Civil War.* Boston, Massachusetts: Beacon Press, 1989.

Zolberg, Aristide R. *A Nation by Design: Immigration Policy in the Fashioning of America.* Boston, Massachusetts: Harvard University Press, 2006.

RESOURCE NOTES
AND ACKNOWLEDGMENTS

RESOURCE NOTES: A book like this one is built not just upon my own research but on the tireless work of career historians. These researchers can spend a professional lifetime immersed in a topic or period of history that may become the focus of my own work for at most a few years. It would be impossible to write the way I do without having access to these scholarly examinations of history. A complete bibliography of cited sources is included in this book, but I would like to call attention to selected key works here, as well.

In the course of writing this book, one historian—Roger Daniels—emerged as a leading source for the study of U.S. immigration. Two key works by him, *Coming to America* and *Guarding the Golden Door,* provided the foundation for my own research. Even beyond these books, it seemed that everywhere I turned I found more work by Roger Daniels, and I owe a debt of gratitude to him for his exhaustive scholarship. His mastery of immigration statistics, understanding of the patterns of immigration, and skill as a writer make his works a pleasure to explore.

The two previously mentioned books and two others by Roger Daniels—*Asian America* and *Not Like Us*—provided valuable background for the opening chapter of this book, "Excluded." Two other historians provided helpful sources about the exclusion and harassment of Chinese immigrants, too. They were *The Huddled Masses* by Alan M. Kraut and Benson Tong's *The Chinese Americans.*

I conducted three independent research projects in order to write the three nonfiction short stories that form the core of this book (Chapters 2-4). Thus the research and writing of each story mimicked the process I would follow for a book-length project on one integrated theme. I identified the focus of my topic, amassed a reading list, tracked down primary source material that supported the project (from photo research to newspaper clippings to oral histories), and documented my research on hundreds of notecards. At times it seemed that I was writing multiple books, not one. I needed to understand the political climate

of post-World War I for the "Deportation" chapter, examine the refugee situation in Nazi-occupied Europe for "Denied," and master the geography of internment camps for "Detained," for example. Each thread of research led me to a separate story, but each story became part of an integrated theme about the dark side of U.S. immigration policy.

Most fascinating of all became the connectedness of these themes not just to one another but to additional incidents in our nation's history—right up to current events unfolding around us now. I love this aspect of history, the way it becomes organic—alive and integrated, with threads of the history we live through every day joining up to echoes and patterns from the past. I find this integrated view of history comforting and full of hope. Surely we can learn and grow by expanding our sense of place in history.

Historians such as Candace Falk *(Love, Anarchy, and Emma Goldman* and *Emma Goldman, A Documentary History of the American Years)*, Alice Wexler *(Emma Goldman in America* and *Emma Goldman in Exile)*, and Regin Schmidt *(Red Scare: FBI and the Origins of Anticommunism in the United States)* provided invaluable scholarly insights for my work on Chapter 2, "Deported." I particularly appreciated the recent scholarship of Regin Schmidt whose work examined newly declassified government documents from the Federal Bureau of Investigation. His research reminds us of how the historian's work—like the scientist's—is never complete. There are always more discoveries out there to be made. Period newspaper clippings about Emma Goldman and Alexander Berkman provided a fascinating contrast to the comprehensive work of historians. The dislike, bias, and mistrust of the era screams from the headlines and blocks of type in papers like the *New York Times.* The digitizing of newspaper archives by the *Times* and other papers makes accessing these resources that much easier, although the Internet will never be able to capture the value of immersing oneself in original documents.

I enjoyed the thrill of on-site research during my work on Chapter 3, "Denied," during a pair of visits to the United States Holocaust Memorial Museum in Washington, D.C. I was able to watch a videotape there of an extended oral history interview with Herbert Karliner, and I paged through the museum's numerous albums of photographs that document the voyage of the *St. Louis* and the lives of its passengers. A portion of these images may be viewed on the museum's website, too. (See the accompanying resource guide for ideas on how to access this and other background information related to this book.) I could not have completed my research without Sarah A. Ogilvie and Scott Miller's book *Refuge Denied*. Their decade of research into the fates of the *St. Louis* passengers was impressive and invaluable. Once again newspaper clippings—in this case available online from the *Washington Post*—provided important insights into the period.

For Chapter 4, "Detained," I turned to the autobiography of Mary Matsuda Gruenewald, *Looking Like the Enemy,* to examine the human dimension behind the wartime internments of Japanese Americans. In addition, I returned to Roger Daniels, who has written extensively about Asian immigration, for historical perspective on the detentions (see works previously cited). Other valuable resources included an anthology of scholarly articles edited by Kay Saunders and Roger Daniels. I made valuable research visits to places like the Manzanar National Historic Site in California, an internment camp property, and the Japanese American National Museum in Los Angeles, too.

For Chapter 5, "Exploited," I returned to the previously cited historical surveys by Roger Daniels and sought new books that captured the experiences of Mexican immigrants. I found *Mexican Americans/American Mexicans* by Matt S. Meier and Feliciano Ribera to be especially valuable, as were contemporary newspaper articles.

This book touches on places I have visited at various points during my life. In addition to sites noted above, I have walked in the paths of immigrants from Chinatowns in San Francisco and New York, to the Ellis Island Immigration Museum, to the Tenement Museum of lower Manhattan, to the National Japanese American Memorial in Washington, D.C. These touchstone visits enriched my connection to the stories of this book. Even periodic trips to the Statue of Liberty—including a childhood glimpse from the statue's crown of the New York City harbor—resonated through my examination of immigration history.

In addition, several trips to Washington, D.C., offered opportunities for on-site archival research with this specific project in mind. Beyond the previously mentioned work at the U.S. Holocaust Memorial Museum, I spent a number of days reviewing images in the Prints and Photographs Division of the Library of Congress. I find so much more than the illustrations for my books during this sort of research. Photographs reveal details that may never have been recorded in a text: a tidbit as simple as the playing of ping-pong on the decks of the *St. Louis,* for example, or one as sobering as the shell-shocked faces of Japanese Americans during their eviction from their homes. Links in the Resource Guide will help readers visit some of these same archives on-line.

ACKNOWLEDGMENTS: Many thanks to Caroline Waddell and other archivists at the U.S. Holocaust Memorial Museum, for sharing their collections with me. I am grateful to the Library of Congress for perennially offering the same courtesy, service, and generosity. I appreciate the cooperation I received from Mary Matsuda Gruenewald and Maureen Michelson at NewSage Press regarding the reproduction of her family photos in this book. A full listing of illustrations credits accompanies this back matter.

I owe appreciation to Professor Roger Daniels, Mary Matsuda Gruenewald, and Herb Karliner for reading relevant sections of this book during its production. Members of my children's book-writing critique group—Georgia Beaverson, Pam Beres, Judy Bryan, Elizabeth Fixmer, Kathleen Petrella, and Jamie Swenson—offered valuable insights during early drafts of the writing process. Thank you. As always, the gifted team at National Geographic Children's Books helped transform my manuscript into a polished, gorgeous book. Many thanks to my editor Jennifer Emmett, designer Marty Ittner, illustrations editor Lori Epstein, design director Bea Jackson, and Nancy Laties Feresten who directs the whole creative symphony. I greatly appreciate the supportive work of book production and marketing staff members, too.

I owe endless appreciation to my sons Sam and Jake for living through another book and for supporting the way that book-life has become part of our family life. Finally, thanks to the older generations, from my parents all the way back to those ancestral British and German immigrants who rooted my fate in America. They stand behind me as I write and explore.

CITATIONS AND ILLUSTRATIONS CREDITS

FOREWORD AND INTRODUCTION

OPENING POEM: p. 6, Emma Lazarus. "The New Colossus" (engraved on commemorative plaque, Statue of Liberty National Monument).

RAISED QUOTE: p. 8, Franklin D. Roosevelt: "Nations, like individuals, make mistakes….correct them." (Daniels, 2004: p. 92).

CHAPTER 1—EXCLUDED

OPENING QUOTE: p. 12, verse by Thomas Bailey Aldrich: "Wide open and unguarded…wild motley throng." (Daniels, 2002: p. 275).

RAISED QUOTE: p. 16, Albert Johnson: "Our capacity to maintain…alien blood." (Daniels, 2004: p. 55).

TEXT: p. 13, Benjamin Franklin: "be so numerous… Anglifying them." (Daniels, 2004: p. 8); p. 17, Henry George: "armed men marshaled for civil war." (Daniels, 1988: p. 40); p. 17, Charles Sumner: "The greatest peril…its great ideals." (Daniels, 1988: p. 43) and "in imagination; it is illusion, not a reality." (Daniels, 2004: p. 15); p. 21, Rock Springs *Independent:* "Let the demand go up….MUST GO." (Daniels, 1988: p. 62); p. 21, Jury report: "a single criminal act…white person that day." (Daniels, 1988: p. 62); p. 21, Oregon rancher: "I guess if they had killed…turned the men loose." (Daniels, 1988: p. 64); p. 22, Wu Ting-fang: "Why can't you be….Chinese had votes?" (Daniels, 1988: p. 93).

CHAPTER 2—DEPORTED

OPENING QUOTE: p. 24, Emma Goldman: "I myself feel….nowhere at home." (Drinnon: p. xi).

RAISED QUOTE: p. 31, Leonard Wood: "They should be put…should be Hell." (Wexler, 1989: p. 10).

PHOTO CAPTIONS: p. 24, Emma Goldman: "We were photographed…like convicted criminals." (Goldman, 1931, Vol. Two: p. 715); p. 31, *New York Times:* "Emma Goldman is not a woman. She is a force." (Thompson: 1909, *New York Times* Sunday Magazine, p. 7); p. 31, Emma Goldman: "The more opposition I encountered…my element." (Wexler, 1989: p. 11); p. 32, J. Edgar Hoover: "two notorious characters…. somewhat unsettled country." (Schmidt: p. 262).

TEXT: p. 29, Alexander Berkman, excerpt from *The ABC of Anarchism:* "Anarchists have no monopoly…a part of the struggle." (Fellner, 2005: p. 270); p. 30, No-Conscription League: "We will fight….ordered to fight." (Glassgold: p. 398); pp. 30-32, Judge Julius Mayer: "For such people as these…no place in our country." ("Convict Berkman and Miss Goldman": p. 8); pp. 34-35, Harry Weinberger, attorney for Emma Goldman and Alexander Berkman: "the present hysteria" and "justice to even…unpopular views at the most unpopular time." ("Deportation Death is Berkman's Plea"); p. 35, J. Edgar Hoover: "beyond doubt, two of the most dangerous anarchists…. result in undue harm." (Department of Justice correspondence, August 23, 1919, National Archives and Records Administration); p. 36, Pamphlet on deportation: "if still alive and of foreign birth…would be threatened by deportation." (Anarchy Archives web page, pitzer.edu); p. 37, Lawyers' declaration: "utterly illegal acts" and "have caused widespread suffering… our country to disgrace." (Schmidt: p. 307); p. 41, Emma Goldman: "You are still free….shoot you down in the streets." ("Emma Goldman, Anarchist, Dead").

CHAPTER 3—DENIED

OPENING QUOTE: p. 42, Josef Joseph: "What started as a voyage of freedom is now a voyage of doom." (Ogilvie and Miller: p. 23).

RAISED QUOTE: p. 50, Adolf Gruenthal: "Not knowing where we are heading is a terrible fate." (Ogilvie and Miller: p. 124).

PHOTO CAPTIONS: p. 42, Captain Gustav Schröder: "Everyone seems convinced…Germany again." (Thomas and Witts: p. 64); p. 46, Captain Gustav Schröder: "Beautiful weather…long sea voyages." (Thomas and Witts: p. 64); p. 49, Herbert Karliner: "but *mañana* never came." (Ogilvie and Miller: p. 21); p. 50, David Lawrence, editor, The U.S. News: "outcry of….love our fellow men." (Lawrence: p. 14).

TEXT: p. 44, Herb Karliner: "I was a boy who wanted to see the world." (Oral history interview conducted by Joe Unger, Holocaust Documentation and Education Center, Miami, Florida, 1985); p. 44, Herb Karliner: "First [Jews] were ordered off the sidewalks….No Jews allowed." (Ogilvie and Miller: p. 38); p. 47, Diary entry: "The sky is dark blue….It's like a dream." (Thomas and Witts: p. 142); p. 51, Liesel Joseph Loeb: "America was a magic word….America would not let us down." (Ogilvie and Miller: p. 23); p. 52, Liesel Joseph: "The children of the *St. Louis*…rescuing them out of deepest despair." (Illustration, United States Holocaust Museum photo archives); p. 59, Herb Karliner and companion: "You know what I cannot understand?....because of us they let them in." (Gerhart: p. C1).

CHAPTER 4—DETAINED

OPENING QUOTE: p. 60, Mary Matsuda Gruenewald (MMG): "Our train rumbled….Uncertainty was all we knew." (Gruenewald: p. 46).

RAISED QUOTE: p. 66, Milton Eisenhower: "When the war is over…may have been done." (Daniels, 1988: p. 227).

PHOTO CAPTIONS: p. 62, MMG: "I was old enough…like a lost child." (Gruenewald: p. 39); p. 73, MMG: "I didn't know…in this country." (Gruenewald: p. 138); p. 77, Harry S. Truman: "You fought not only…and you have won." (Gruenewald: p. 188).

TEXT: pp. 61-62, MMG: "It was my last carefree morning….American teenager." (Gruenewald: p. 2); p. 63, Lieut. General John L. DeWitt: "A Jap's a Jap….an American citizen." (Hata and Hata: p. 223); p. 64, MMG: "That fateful day…in the living room." (Gruenewald: p. 26); p. 65, Mr. Matsuda: "We'll do whatever…in spite of everything." (Gruenewald: p. 6); p. 65, Refrain: "*Shigata ganai.*" "It can't be helped." (Gruenewald: 223); p. 67, Spectator: "Get outta here, you God damn Japs!" (Gruenewald: 44); p. 69, MMG: "My deep fear…kill us all." (Gruenewald: p. 72); p. 72, MMG: "Are these trick questions?" "was confusing…among the internees." (Gruenewald: pp. 115-117); p. 72, Mr. Matsuda: "It is important….I choose to vote 'Yes Yes.'" (Gruenewald: p. 129); p. 73, Yoneichi Matsuda: "My 'Yes Yes' decision….loyalty to the United States." (Gruenewald: p. 131); p. 73, MMG: "Although I knew….bully in the schoolyard." (Gruenewald: p. 132); p. 74, MMG: "It took me more than 50 years….Dissent is an essential expression of democracy." (Gruenewald: p. 133); p. 76, President Gerald R. Ford: "We know now…are loyal Americans"; "an honest reckoning"; "our national mistakes." (Hata and Hata: p. 229); p. 78, Manzanar exhibit: "Who were these people like?" (author's notes); p. 78, Roger Daniels: "is an ironic and disgraceful aspect…was freedom." (Daniels, 1988: p. 187); pp. 78–79, Roger Daniels: "Could it happen again?" (Daniels, 2000, edited vol.: p. 182); p. 79, Roger Daniels: "to react against….have dark skin." (Daniels, 2000, edited vol.: p. 184).

CHAPTER 5—EXPLOITED

OPENING QUOTE: p. 80, Ranch foreman: "When we want you, we'll call you; when we don't—git." (McWilliams: p. 126).

RAISED QUOTE: p. 86, Charles Teague: "[Mexicans are] naturally adapted….good-natured and happy." (Teague: pp. 141–42).

PHOTO CAPTIONS: p. 80, Mexican worker: "I have worked…my broken body." (Library of Congress, Prints and Photographs, caption information).

TEXT: p. 85, Sign: "No niggers, Mexicans, or dogs allowed." (Meier and Ribera: p. 150); p. 85, Indiana immigrant: "They gave you a choice, starve or go back to Mexico." (Daniels, 2004: p. 64).

AFTERWORD

RAISED QUOTE: p. 92, Lyndon B. Johnson: "Our tradition…going to be upheld." (Daniels, 2004: p. 198).

PHOTO CAPTIONS: p. 94, Wu Ting-fang: "Why can't you be fair?" (Daniels, 1988: p. 93).

TEXT: p. 95, George Washington: "The bosom of America….all nations and religions." (Daniels, 2004: p. 7).

ILLUSTRATIONS CREDITS

Grateful acknowledgment is made for the use of images from the following sources. Abbreviations used below are: LC (courtesy the Library of Congress Prints and Photographs Division), MMG (courtesy Mary Matsuda Gruenewald and NewSage Press), and USHMM (courtesy the United States Holocaust Memorial Museum, the views or opinions expressed in this book and the context in which the images are used, do not necessarily reflect the views or policy of, nor imply approval or endorsement by the USHMM). Front cover top inset, USHMM 24795; middle inset, MMG; bottom inset, LC-DIG-ggbain-00751; background, Istockphoto.com; p. 1, USHMM 18528; pp. 2-3, Bettmann/Corbis BE050533; p. 6, Justin Lane/epa/Corbis 42-15938994; p. 7, LC-USZ62-91172; p. 8, LC-USZ62-59860; p. 11, LC-USZC2-784; p. 12 inset, LC-USZ62-56607; pp. 12-13 background, LC-USZ62-110967; p. 15, LC-USZC2-1242; p. 16, LC-USZ62-107167; p. 19, LC-USZC2-1213; p. 20, LC-USZ62-96518; pp. 22-23, (LC) PAN US GEOG - California no. 238; p. 24 left inset, LC-DIG-ggbain-29922; p. 24 right inset, LC-USZ62-40636; pp. 24-25 background, LC-USZ62-40635; pp. 26-27 background, LC-USZ62-77926; p. 27 inset, LC-USZ62-53176; p. 28, LC-USZ62-33541; p. 31, Bettmann/Corbis BE033127; p. 32, LC-USZ62-92411; pp. 34-35 background, Bettmann/Corbis U100987INP; p. 35, LC-DIG-ggbain-24437; p. 39, Bettmann/Corbis VV6779; p. 40 inset, International Institute of Social History BG/A5/525; p. 40 background, LC-USZ62-61671; p. 42 inset, USHMM 22523; p. 42 background, USHMM 31683; p. 45, USHMM 28472; p. 46 left inset, USHMM 88364; p. 46 right inset, USHMM 38581; p. 46 background, USHMM 31853; p. 49, Bettmann/Corbis BE037830; p. 50, USHMM 03184; pp. 52-53, USHMM 76528, and courtesy Centre d'Etudes et de Documentation Guerre et Sociétés Contemporaines, Belgium; p. 57 upper, USHMM 28473; p. 57 lower, USHMM 28471; p. 58 inset, USHMM 30787; p. 58 background, USHMM 00370; p. 60 inset, LC-DIG-ppmsc-09965; pp. 60-61 background, LC-USZ62-133631; p. 62, upper, MMG; p. 62, lower, MMG; p. 65, LC-USZ6-1837; p. 66, LC-USZ6-1830; p. 69, Oregon Historical Society 44617; p. 70 upper, LC-USZ62-133819; p. 70 lower, LC-USZ62-127899; p. 70 background, MMG; p. 74, MMG; pp. 76-77, The Mariner's Museum/Corbis, US001330; p. 78, Reuters/Corbis UT0081987; p. 80 inset, LC-DIG-ppmsca-19156-0038; pp. 80-81 background, LC-USW3-026249-D; pp. 82-83, LC-USZ62-41533; p. 84, LC-DIG-ppmsca-19156-0025; p. 86, LC-DIG-ppmsca-19156-0001; p. 89, LC-USW33-031865-C; p. 90, LC-USW3-026258-D; p. 92, LC-USZ62-21220; p. 94, Underwood & Underwood/Corbis, BE078166; p. 96 (1819), Corbis, IH162587; p. 96 (1889), LC-USZ62-63658; p. 97 (1850s), LC-USZ62-56607; p. 97 (1869), Bettmann/Corbis BE065953; p. 97 (1907), National Archives 90-G-125-29; p. 98 (1919), LC-USZ62-40635; p. 98 (1933), Keystone/Corbis 42-17759393; p. 98 (1941), Bettmann/Corbis U630050EACME; p. 98 (1942), LC-USZ62-88338; p. 99 (1926), USHMM 28469; p. 99 (1940), Bettmann/Corbis BE033963; p. 100 (1943), MMG; p. 100 (1945 upper), John Van Hasselt/Corbis Sygma, 0000304422-039; p. 100 (1945 lower), LC-USW33-031866-C; p. 101 (1950), LC-USZ62-117122; p. 101 (1980), Bettmann/Corbis, BE023837; p. 101 (2003), Ramin Talaie/Corbis, DWF15-924371; p. 112, LC-USZ62-137829; back cover, LC-USZ62-116223.

INDEX

PUBLISHED BY THE NATIONAL
GEOGRAPHIC SOCIETY
John M. Fahey, Jr., *President and Chief
Executive Officer*
Gilbert M. Grosvenor, *Chairman of the Board*
Tim T. Kelly, *President, Global Media Group*
John Q. Griffin, *President, Publishing*
Nina D. Hoffman, *Executive Vice President;
President, Book Publishing Group*

PREPARED BY THE BOOK DIVISION
Nancy Laties Feresten, *Vice President, Editor in
Chief, Children's Books*
Bea Jackson, *Director of Design
and Illustrations, Children's Books*
Amy Shields, *Executive Editor, Series, Children's Books*
Jennifer Emmett, *Executive Editor,
Reference and Solo, Children's Books*
Carl Mehler, *Director of Maps*

STAFF FOR THIS BOOK
Jennifer Emmett, *Editor*
Bea Jackson, *Art Director*
Lori Epstein, *Illustrations Editor*
Marty Ittner, *Designer*
Sven Dolling, *Map Research and Production*
Jennifer A. Thornton, *Managing Editor*
Grace Hill, *Associate Managing Editor*
R. Gary Colbert, *Production Director*
Lewis Bassford, *Production Manager*
Susan Borke, *Legal and Business Affairs*

MANUFACTURING AND
QUALITY MANAGEMENT
Christopher A. Liedel, *Chief Financial Officer*
Phillip L. Schlosser, *Vice President*
Chris Brown, *Technical Director*
Monika Lynde, *Manager*

Founded in 1888, the National
Geographic Society is one of the
largest nonprofit scientific and
educational organizations in the
world. It reaches more than 285
million people worldwide each
month through its official journal,
National Geographic, and its four other
magazines; the National Geographic Channel;
television documentaries; radio programs;
films; books; videos and DVDs; maps; and
interactive media. National Geographic has
funded more than 8,000 scientific research
projects and supports an education program
combating geographic illiteracy.

For more information, please call
1-800-NGS LINE (647-5463) or write to
the following address:

National Geographic Society
1145 17th Street N.W., Washington, D.C.
20036-4688 U.S.A.

Visit us online at www.nationalgeographic.
com/books

For librarians and teachers: www.
ngchildrensbooks.org

More for kids from National Geographic: kids.
nationalgeographic.com

For information about special discounts for
bulk purchases, please contact
National Geographic Books Special Sales:
ngspecsales@ngs.org

For rights or permissions inquiries, please
contact National Geographic Books Subsidiary
Rights: ngbookrights@ngs.org

Immigrants who appear to be waving hello to the Statue of Liberty are in fact waving goodbye: They are being deported as illegal aliens in 1952.